I'M CHASING MYSELF

I'M CHASING MYSELF

A YOUNG BOY'S JOURNEY TO REKINDLE THE WONDER AND CURIOSITY HE ONCE HAD ABOUT HIS WORLD.

WINONA RAJAMOHAN

NEW DEGREE PRESS

COPYRIGHT © 2019 WINONA RAJAMOHAN

I'M CHASING MYSELF

*A Young Boy's Journey to Rekindle the Wonder and
Curiosity He Once Had About His World.*

ISBN   978-1-64137-366-1   *Paperback*

          978-1-64137-712-6   *Ebook*

To my parents, thank you for giving me a reason to wake up with a smile every day even when I don't want to. Your love and support lifts me up constantly, even from halfway across the world.

CONTENTS

NOTE FROM THE AUTHOR

——

My most prominent memory of wanting to write a book started when I was in elementary school. I got a copy of *How to Write a Book for Dummies* from the nearby bookstore and spent weeks in front of an old beat-up computer writing a chapter. I bound the pages and slipped it under my parent's bedroom door. It was such an exciting moment for me, but I always struggled with one thing—seeing a story through until the end.

Writing this story was different. I knew I had a story that could be seen through the end, because I was at a point in my life where I had seen so many of my own personal experiences begin and end. I'm a dreamer, a girl that romanticizes the highs and lows of self-discovery and how connected that journey is to the relationships with people around you. But I reached a state of mind where the need for companionship and reliance on others was something that I refused to accept. I moved halfway across the world from my home and everyone I loved, hoping that independence would be my route to satisfaction. I was wrong.

Living continents away from the sights and traditions that I had spent twenty years of my life, I realized that my accomplishments were achievable, but there was still always going to be something missing. I was always so against routine, desperately searching for something new, but throwing away your anchor doesn't mean that your boat won't sit firmly on stagnant water even just for a second. My book begins with my reminiscing of sights, smells, behaviors and traits that I remember vividly although they're no longer a part of my everyday life. It begins with an ode to friendship and family, but a desperate cry for self-fulfillment. It explores the intersections of youthful problems and how they are mistreated by others. "You'll grow out of it," is the claim that I want to argue because the pain and pressure felt during this process leaves scars when treated with no urgency.

My romantic side of life had come to a standstill at one point, tainted by the weight of wavering mental health and a longing to find an escape. This book was my escape, and it paints a picture of this process in finding that escape. It's a pat on the back to any young person who has felt as though they were free-falling, but who also refused to hold onto the hands reaching out to catch them. It's a reminder to everybody that you can't do things on your own, and that it's okay to ask for help. I learned that running away from genuine relationships and loving bonds isn't the answer, independence is not solitude.

I want my readers to take away that same message too.

CHAPTER 1

OUR SPOT

———

"I swear Gry, if you burn the hair off my knees again with that thing I will throw you out this open window," Kivo said.

He leaned over to place his lips around the cigarette in Gryme's fingertips anyway. Kivo leaned his small frame back onto the seat with ease. He was skinny with long limbs, most of the weight on his body coming from the extremely over-sized Vetements t-shirt he was wearing. The white piece of fabric had rows of scribbled black words on it with nothing else, but it probably cost more than all the clothes everyone else was wearing put together.

The car was too small and the air conditioning never worked, so the windows were always rolled down to let the humid wind in. Kivo always sat by a window, Cassie and Mitch in the middle and Mo on the other end. Their foreheads would be sticky with sweat, but the nicotine rush always got them through the discomfort of bumping shoulders, occasional mosquito bites, and the stench off Gryme's unsanitary clothes.

"Jesus…you have a year's worth of food crumbs and stains on you," Mo muttered under his breath. Gryme yelled back at him to shut up.

Mo was right. All I could smell was a mix of salty and sweet, a sharp twist that made me scrunch my nose on impulse. It was the saltiness of sweat, and the sweet twang reminded me of barbecue sauce. It made my head spin, my fingers gripping harder on the steering wheel while my friends persisted with their bickering.

The road ahead was dark. The dim yellow hues of the street lights were diminished by their pulsated flickering. If this road wasn't so familiar to us, I might have found it a little scary. My head wasn't in the right place to drive anyway, but it was a Friday night tradition to head down to our spot and hang out there.

"Hey Jess you good? You haven't said a word this whole ride," Cassie said softly, leaning forward to give me a light squeeze on my shoulder.

"I'm just a little tired, I was helping my mom lift furniture and stuff all day," I answered, turning my head over to give her a little smile.

It wasn't too big of a lie. I wasn't lifting furniture but I was helping my mom lift her spirits just a little bit. It was my brother's birthday today, and she had brought home a cake and called me downstairs this morning to sing a happy birthday song for him. The funny thing is, he wasn't home. He ran away actually, a couple of days after his birthday last year.

On most days, I can handle keeping my brother out of my mind. I stop wondering where he could be and if he was safe. It wasn't that easy today, not with my mother sitting at the dining table eating his birthday cake by herself. All these questions in my head felt heavy, like they had a hand around my neck. I didn't feel like leaving the house to drive or see anyone tonight, but I decided it was the best way to keep myself busy. Maybe I could sort this uneasiness in my chest when we reached our spot—it always helps.

* * *

The faint tinge of sea salt laced through the air at all points of the day, even though the ocean wasn't too close to the heart of the town. Traces of its scent always found its way back onto the busy streets, perhaps because they were often left on the clothes of high school kids who were always sneaking out in the dark of the night.

I snatched the car keys off my mother's nightstand, quietly promising to only leave her home alone for just a little while as I gently pulled the comforters higher over her small shoulders. I always kept a bottle of air freshener in her car trunk to hide the scent brooding out of little plastic bags stuffed in Kivo's front jean pockets.

We would drive to our spot every week with a packed backseat. They didn't mind, but it made for less than ideal circumstances for the already hot and sticky night.

There was a basket of my mom's laundry piled on the passenger seat. They were adamant that squeezing everyone in the backseat was a much better option than trying to move a pile topped with her underwear. Gryme, wearing that one green hoodie that was probably never washed, lay across the laps of the other four in the backseat with him. His hand was hanging up in the air to keep the ash from his lit cigarette from falling onto the bare skin of everyone's laps.

"Was that stop light always working? I thought it had been busted for years. It's crazy how much we don't notice these little things," Mo said, squeezing his eyes together to look out onto the next street.

Mo was a cross between being a dreamer and someone that was just spaced out most of the time. His heavy-lidded eyes made him look like he had just woken up from a nap as he tried to cup his fingers around them for a closer look.

"Why do you make everything sound like a scene from a movie? It's a stop light, they break and they get fixed all the time," Gryme said in a sing-song voice as Cassie and Mitchel squeezed over to the window.

The streets in town were still brightly lit even in the middle of the night. Store owners would gather in front of their chained doors on plastic chairs, lighting cigarettes in their stained old shirts to talk about their worst customers of the day.

A soccer game was always on in the restaurants that stayed open all night. That's where we would usually find the rest of our schoolmates pouring the tea out of their glasses to replace it with the beer pulled out of someone's backpack. I used to head out to these places a lot with my brother during his first year of high school.

Sometimes we needed our distance from these worn-out buildings, inconsiderate drivers, rude store workers and the heavy disapproval that always weighed down on the shoulders of every face we would walk past on the street. Everyone seemed to look at high school kids like we were stuck in a useless mid-point between being useless and being useful. Everybody looked at us with a face eager to leave this place. We weren't sure where exactly all people would ever think about leaving to. None of them seemed like the type to make it out of this small town. Then again, we knew none of them would ever leave regardless of what they thought. They might just hate us so much because we looked like we could leave this small town.

"You're right, that light was never working. It's weird that they've fixed it now, nobody ever gets on this street now it's practically dead," Mitchel said.

The street was right before the exit out of town. Once making the turn, palm trees would start lining both sides of the road and the path ahead looks like it leads to the end of the world. The gravel beneath the car tires started mixing with sand and washed out twigs, making little crunching sounds that echoed through the still night air. I turned the music down, letting the sound of soft and crashing waves take over.

"Not this song, I want it loud!" Gryme yelled out, jolting right up into the roof of the car and letting orange-speckled ash spread across all the bare skin it could reach.

"I think I'll keep the volume right here, man," I said with a laugh, looking through the front mirror to see the mess unfolding in the backseat alongside Cassie's screaming. As always, it was going to be a loud twenty minutes to get there.

The sand by the water was rough, not the kind of place where we would want to lay a beach towel to get a tan. We walked carefully and slowly from their car to the beach, watching out for shards of beer bottle glasses and moly that were always lying around, sticking upwards.

* * *

It was always silent once we got to the edge of this town, as though the sky and the trees were holding their breath to make way for the water making its way to the shore. We came here for that silence, a silence so crisp that I swear I could hear the sounds of the stars burning in space.

Sometimes we come on weekends, taking the books out of our backpacks and replacing them with cheap bottles of alcohol that we could get from the grocery store behind our school. The place was owned by one of our classmates' old man. He worked Friday nights and we could get him to sneak bottles of whatever we want with a slight increment in price. The kid was a natural businessman.

Sometimes we would come on Mondays straight out of class, meeting at the wire fence by the school soccer field (the one with the big hole that was ripped into by a sick stray dog).

This night felt a little different. First of all it was colder, the sea breeze smelled like fish, but it smelled familiar and they were fine with that. They sat in a straight line facing the water and a broken net strung out at the edge of their feet.

A single spotlight from a ferry on the water kept flashing, casting a single white strobe across a pitch black surface.

"I want one," Jesse would always say. His signature white long sleeves were rolled up to his elbows and the only thing on his shirt was a loud purple graphic of an octopus eating a mermaid. The graffiti-inspired art piece on his chest was so haunting that its pink hues almost shone through the dark.

"What's your reason for tonight?" Cassie asked, grabbing the newly lit cigarette right out of his fingertips and diving the stick bud-first into the sand.

Jesse slid a Marlboro pack out of his pocket without a flinch.

"I don't know, Cassie. I always wanted to count how many rooms are in that thing, how many little hidden pockets can I find in just an hour of walking around a ship? How many doors can I open?"

Cassie had a little smile on her face and he could catch it for a split second when the strobe light fell on her face.

"You're always wanting to find new rooms and open new doors aren't you?" she asked, twisting the soggy net between her toes and laying her back on the sand. The nets were heavy with the smell of salt and seaweed, one end of it hanging loosely over the edge of a small wooden fishing boat a couple of feet away. "Jess we all know you don't want to stay here."

I knew this conversation was coming. I never doubted that my best friends would be the first ones to catch me in my tracks if something was a little off. I know I've been making them feel uneasy with how I would skip soccer games to stay home and watch TV. I could feel everyone's eyes on me and I didn't need to look to know.

"If you're bored of the beach you know we could always switch it up, you can just tell us," Lenny said, offering him an open bag of chips.

"You were the one always telling us not to be like all the sad adults that look like they hate everything, and now your face looks exactly like theirs," Cassie said. "What's going on, Jesse?"

I didn't know what to say. I really didn't have anything to say. I just know that I didn't want to wake up to the creaking of my busted ceiling fan. I didn't want to step out of the house each morning to hear my sick neighbor rolling her wheelchair around asking me to believe in Jesus Christ. Faith sounds corny, I don't buy it. The point is I just felt unsatisfied (unsatisfied without an ounce of clarity about why).

All I could see when I stared at the dark waters out in front of me were racing images. They were transitioning so fast from one to the other that they looked more like blotches of paint. It was making my head hurt and I wished that it would stop. But every now and then I would see something that I like, coming at me in white flashes.

I could see flowers, small little red ones that I used to pluck out of bushes when I was a kid and suck on to get the nectar out. My mom always yelled at me for doing it, she would tell me that it was dirty and filled with bee droppings and that I was going to die. My brother would always just pull more of them out and split them evenly between us.

"Bees don't even have droppings, she's lying," he would say. They were called Ixora flowers, and they grew everywhere around the park outside my house. Sucking on the nectar was a thing with the kids for some reason. They always had such a bright red color, the most vibrant things against a backdrop of worn out shop lots and a thin layer of haze that was always in the air. This town always smelled like smoke. I could smell it even by the ocean.

I could see images of a soccer ball rolling toward an exciting jumping dog by the school fence. The dog used to be really friendly, and then a few months later we saw it crouched up by the same fence looking so uncontrollably angry and skinny, maybe the dog was sick. Maybe the dog was sick from the smoke.

Another image flashed by of me waking up in the middle of the night to the sound of crickets and some of my school-mates playing poker. They would park their bikes under a tree next to my window. The tree had a bunch of old wooden chairs that somebody had left years ago. The rain and sun had done its damage to them, and I'm pretty sure they're rotting and not safe to be sat on. But this was the best spot to sneak out to, right in the central point from where all of them lived. That was their spot.

I could see all these moments in my life and I could see how happy and comfortable I was with all the little imperfections. The imperfections built character and they made this place feel more like a home because they were imperfections that only we could understand. Imperfections only the people in this town got to see.

But it didn't feel that way anymore now when I think about them. The imperfections that once felt comfortable were start-ing to become painful. I didn't look forward to them, I just wanted to break them apart and crumble them into pieces. I felt like I was being engulfed in something—a mix of curiosity, anger and a longing for something new. I couldn't put my finger on what that something was, does frustration really just pop up out of nowhere? Is anxiety just a switch that the wind can blow over and flip without me doing anything about it?

Cassie was right about me losing myself, but tonight just wasn't the night for me to talk about it. I just needed to get out of there and walk around a little bit. The salt in the breeze was making it harder for me to breathe.

* * *

"Another night another dramatic departure," Gryme's singsong voice echoed through the empty beach as he watched Jess' silhouette slip away from sight. "I know this whole man-in-distress thing is getting kind of weird coming from him, but I don't know if your confrontation is working that well, Cassie."

"Well, you just let him walk away while you sat there smoking! If you think I'm doing it wrong, why don't you do something for once?" Cassie shouted as she stood up, her voice getting louder with each passing word.

Gryme simply raised both his palms, mocking a sign of defeat. Mitchel tugged on her arm, motioning for her to sit down as he shot a glare at Gryme.

"I'm just saying that if we think that Jess wants to be this other person and grow up, be more independent or whatever, it doesn't mean we're losing him, you know what I mean?" Gryme added nonchalantly, putting his cigarette out on the top of an empty beer can.

"It's weird that I'm saying this but Gry's right," Kivo said, giving Gryme a firm grasp on the shoulder. Mo, Mitchel and Cassie stared at Gryme with their mouths slightly agape. For somebody that usually only spoke in terms of viral tweets and dubstep song lyrics to lighten up the mood, given the situation, that sentence carried a lot of weight.

Kivo, on the other hand, spent the most time with Gryme out of everyone given the fact that they lived two houses away from each other. Through their walks to school together and their equally bold plans to sneak out of school during lunch to grab a hot dog from the other side of the street, Kivo had come to learn over the years about how much Gryme depended on this little circle of friends.

He was at their homes more than he was at his and he had more meals taken care of by all their parents compared to his own. Gryme was the first one to notice how Jesse had stopped coming out with them on most nights and he was the first one to bring it up. Kivo was sure that it bothered him more than he would like to admit when Jesse merely brushed his comment off with a small shrug before walking home.

"I get it. I mean, I don't think we understand Jesse's feelings enough to try and stop him from being whatever he wants to be," Mitchel said, turning to look at everyone in the group but letting his gaze linger a little longer on a very agitated-looking Cassie. He was more concerned about making sure that she was keeping her calm, because the last thing they needed at this point was another person storming off into the woods (especially not someone who would be as hard to track as a petite brown-eyed girl with a temper that could set off an army).

"We don't know what he wants but we know who Jesse is, who he has been all these years, and the Jesse we know loves exploring the world around him, he has the weirdest hobbies, he's a hopeless romantic and he loves being just as emotionally attached as he is emotionally vacant."

The rest of them nodded slowly.

"That was really accurate," Mo said with a chuckle. "I just thought of something that might solve all our problems. How about we bring our little Jessy boy on a surprise trip this weekend?"

CHAPTER 2

CROSSROADS

———

I could hear the sound of shuffling feet in the sand somewhere in the distance behind me. It was a rugged sort of rushed walking; the kind that snapped twigs mercilessly and kicked sand all over the place. The footsteps didn't sound like they were going to be able to catch up to me, it sounded too faint to be anywhere close enough. The night was still so silent, even with all the rustling tree tops in the wind and the crashing waves, so silent that I could probably catch the sound of toes dipping in the sand from a mile away.

I could imagine Cassie back on the beach trying to hush up the rest of the boys and to stop them from running after me. That's even if anyone did try to chase after me. I wouldn't have felt the obligation for them to, especially considering the distance I've been putting between me and them. This was probably the first car ride where I didn't join in on conversations or try to make jokes. I really couldn't bring myself to break my silence, or to lift my focus off the road ahead. I still had fingernail marks on my palm from gripping the steering wheel too hard.

I don't even know why I got up and decided to walk away in the first place. I scanned my eyes around me and everything was getting pitch black. The only source of light was coming from a full moon tucked behind the shadows of palm tree leaves. I stopped for a moment just to stare at it, amazed at how it was lighting everything up in a way that was so strong yet so subtle. It was reflecting sunlight after all, if I remember correctly from one of my classes. The silence was starting to get a little uncomfortable and I realized that maybe I would much rather be looking at the blinking ferry spotlight in the water instead of being out here.

But what's done is done. I got on my feet and I walked away. I was pretty angry at myself just thinking about how often I seemed to react like this. It was always too easy for me to shut everyone out, heading further and further down the opposite direction of things I needed to confront. I was good at closing myself off—the self that was confused, the self that was most desperate for answers and validation and expression. Ignoring that vulnerability was something I had perfected after uncomfortable times of practice.

I despised the appeal people had for my character. I was sick of being the boy with the boisterous laugh and mischievous eyes. I was tired of being so restless and eager for adventure. I also have a bad habit of shaking my leg too much just because I feel like I'm medically inhibited from sitting still. I don't have a diagnosis but I just feel it in my gut. I want to believe that there was more to me than the "energy I bring into the room" as people like to call it. I used to love endless conversation, talking about how people decided on their dreams and what they would do if they failed to reach them. I loved looking into different sets of eyes, watching in real-time as my life lit up with an abundance of different characters.

But right now, I felt like I was standing at the intersection of everyone's lives. I heard their stories, their dreams and aspirations. I watched them pass by me with their successes and their failures, threading along their own paths while I stayed still. I would rather fall than stay stagnant, falling gives me a reason to keep walking forward. Why does it feel like my feet are planted to the ground? Maybe it was my lust for life, one patched together with movie scenes and song lyrics about having my heart broken by people I never realized had my heart in the first place. Maybe I couldn't move because my purpose was to be a stop along the way for everyone I meet. A check point if they needed to be snapped out of reality and pulled into a teenage twilight zone of possibilities. Do dreamers really go nowhere?

When I was younger, this town was all I knew. I believed that life was made in every corner of these streets. From the ice-cream cart that drove past my elementary school each day with the chimpanzee-sounding honk, to the broken shopping cart by the parking lot behind the library that looked so straight out of Tumblr that high school kids would plan months in advance to have their first kiss there.

I just wanted to note that I only took a week and a half to plan my kiss by the way. Anne was a great girl. Her hair smelled like coconut clusters and almonds, and her skin smelled like cocoa butter. Her lips were a little rough and cracked on the edges because she bit them a lot when she was nervous. She couldn't play any instruments and she definitely couldn't sing, but she collected sheet music of her favorite songs just so she could look at the pattern of the notes as they rose and dipped on the page according to the tune of the music. She was a dreamer like me and she left this town two years ago.

I really did believe that I could live out every song lyric movie scene by just walking along these pavements. But I was running out of songs and I was running out of unexplored places. I've been recycling movies and distorting them with horrific visions just so they would be a little different, just so I could feel something.

I had been so lost in my thoughts that I forgot I was still walking through a dark beachside jungle in the middle of the night. I had to pause to take a breath, my hands perched on my knees and my body bent over so I could look down and face the ground. I couldn't see the ground regardless and I just really hoped there were no snakes. I also noticed that my flip-flops were starting to fray at the edges. I kept walking, letting the coarse sand and sharp twigs scratch again the sides of my feet.

"I wonder if any of them are going to come find me," I muttered under my breath, swatting a fly out of my face.

I would be lying if I said I didn't hope to hear pacing footsteps behind me, I wanted to be alone but I wanted to be found. I wanted my friends to find me, as selfish as that may sound.

My friends, my best friends that I would get ice cream with every day after school from that same noisy cart, the same friends that would sneak through the hole in the fence by the field, because there was no place quieter by our homes at midnight to pass a blunt around.

The same friends that knocked on my room door without end for an hour on the day my brother ran away. They knocked until I finally opened the door and they sat around the floor as I lay face down on my bed until I felt too hungry to ignore them anymore.

I didn't talk to them about it, I just wanted food. That was the day the squeak of the fan started to become unbearable. It was the day I walked out of the front door and realized that I couldn't see a world that had much to offer anymore. Everyone was moving on or running away.

My mom's been telling me every night since that day, "Why do I feel like you're going to leave me too?"

Suddenly, a pair of hands covered my eyes. My heart stopped.

And then the smell of lavender sleeping lotion hit my face instantly. I realized I wasn't getting kidnapped and being trafficked to a neighboring island.

"Knew I'd find you here," Cassie said a little too enthusiastically, pouting slightly when I grabbed her hands and pushed them away. "Are you crazy, Cass? You almost killed me with that," I told her, a little too agitated to stop myself from raising my voice.

"Don't act like you weren't hoping for someone to come find you. You're not as tough as you think you are," she said, her face expressionless as she placed a hand firmly on her hip.

I cleared my throat. "Where are the other boys?" I asked. Her face was now right underneath the moon's gentle hues and I noticed how her dark hair was falling in messy waves onto her white tank top. Cassie was always a fighter, one of the boys. I was afraid to admit that sometimes, whenever she ran after me like this, it really does hit me how she's become the strongest woman in my life, someone for me to lean on and hold me up.

"They're in the car," she said. "I'm sorry I pushed you to your edge by saying those things, you know how I am with not knowing the right time and place for things..."

The second half of her sentence was falling into a little whisper before she continued again. "But we can talk about that another day. This was supposed to be a good night for all of us, and a good night doesn't include having you standing here in the dark with all this stinky sand. We're getting burgers, from your favorite stall by the gas station near school. Let's go."

She was a tough one to deal with, but I'm not complaining. She always knew what to say.

"Let's go," I said, draping an arm around her shoulder and walking back toward the beach. Cassie rambled on about how the car didn't have enough fuel and that they were all going to end up pushing the car for the last half a mile on the way.

It was a weird night, but somehow I still ended it feeling grateful. I really was grateful, for many things and people in my life, and I suppose that made me feel worse about the way I kept acting. I had no reason to be this unhappy, but I needed to answer all these questions in my head.

* * *

"You need to aim higher when you throw it, or it's not going to cross the fence!"

We had yet to fall asleep, spending the last two hours trying to drunkenly toss a cotton ball over their neighbor's fence onto her car. It was an ugly looking thing with one busted front light and chipped blood red paint all over the doors. The backseat of the car was always filled with plastic bags, metal rods and clothes from their neighbors driving to and from the hospital so often. The lady was the one that was sick. We didn't know exactly what it was and neither of us really wanted to ask.

We had to admit that we enjoyed seeing the smile on her sunken pale face each morning when she saw us leave for school. She was always wearing a dark colored frock with some sort of weird pattern printed all over it—rubber ducks, Aztec triangles, or even human teeth. I was certain that she was a wild grunge princess back in her younger days. Maybe that's how she found such a charming husband, his eyes warm and doting as we would watch him each day gingerly carry her from the front seat of the ugly red car into her wheelchair before giving her a kiss on the cheek each time without fail.

I took a step back, letting my brother's broad shoulders and tall built frame completely block the sun from touching the top of my head. Dawson was a big guy who only wore tank tops and khaki shorts, the shoes on his feet always rugged with a few frayed holes at the tips of his toes from run-ins with the police. He would always get into trouble for trespassing in the neighborhood and stealing Snicker bars from the local grocery store.

We were on our front porch and it was a little after six in the morning. There were two little bottles of cheap gin lying by our feet. We got them from the same liquor store that my friend's dad owned. It was supposed to have a tinge of lychee but unless lychee was another way to describe kerosene, I doubted that the label was telling them any form of truth.

The sun rose pretty early in the middle of August. It was an odd observation we stumbled upon considering how our humid tropical climate was warm shine and warm rain all year round without much variation in temperature. We took it as a sign to let the nights of August hold our favorite memories. If the sky wasn't going to stay dark as long as we liked, we had to make sure that we did every crazy thing that we could think of fitting into the pitch black of night.

The cotton ball didn't manage to cross the fence yet again, even though Dawson put his heart and soul into leaping off the ground and tumbling down with his head in a daze and his vision blurry. I watched and scoffed as the cotton ball slowly rode its way downward through the air and landed a little over a foot away from where we were sitting.

"Maybe we should give up, man. I can't be on my best game with you around," Dawson sighed, his body sprawled on the cement tiles by their front door as he gazed up at the sky that was turning a brighter shade of blue.

"That's why I'm usually not around you anyway, right?" I asked, a little surprised at how cynical I sounded. I was extremely surprised I said anything at all. Dawson and I had a weird relationship. Over the last couple years, I had finally come to terms with the fact that he was my favorite person in the world and it bothered me that I felt this way. He wasn't the best brother, on most days he ceased to acknowledge the fact that I existed. He would never take a glance at me in school, or if we somehow ended up bumping into each with our friends at the park or mall. But when nobody else was around, he would step into the empty shoes left by my dad and become the fatherly figure I never really had. He would tell me that my posture during assembly was a disaster, and that I should stop letting my friends drag me into doing childish things with them. Outside of the house, he was silent. In the house, in the safety net of our four walls and the bedrooms we've had since we were little kids, he would be my superhero.

I didn't understand it, and now that I'm older, I feel obliged to begin trying.

Dawson looked over at me with his lips pursed, "You know I don't mean to push you away when we're outside the house, it's just the people that we both hang around with…"

"They acted different when I was younger but I'm older now. Alcohol? Weed? My friends do the same thing, what's the big deal?" I was starting to feel my heartbeat accelerate. The first time I realized that Dawson's public persona didn't include the role of being my big brother was when he insisted that we both left to school at different times. Dawson would still put me in a headlock and ruffle my hair before he left, or throw me a granola bar he had from his room's snack stash to make sure I ate something each morning. But once he was out those doors, I was just another face in the crowd eager and in awe to take in the mysterious appeal of Dawson Loo. Tall and big broad shoulders were pretty synonymous to a high school heart-throb. Dawson never paid attention to any of it though, and the people he kept close were four other boys that we had practically grown up with.

"I don't want you around my friends. I don't want them to think that they can talk to you or be closer to you because you're my brother. I don't want you to worry about the things I have to worry about," Dawson said. His voice was strained, caught between the need to scream and the want to whisper. "It's not that they're bad people, I know we do the same things. You really think I'm trying to hide you from drugs and ciggys, come on, this isn't fifty years ago where hiding things means nobody's going to find out."

I was nothing but confused at this point. Wouldn't anyone be? Nothing about anything he's saying makes sense. If he wasn't worried about the bad things his friends were doing then what did he have to hide? Were they murdering people? Were they running some underground illegal ring? Dawson definitely spent too much time doing nothing to do anything criminal-worthy. His friends didn't strike me as the kind of people capable of organizing a scheme (or anything really) either.

"It's the way they make me feel, the way they make me think. They make me question things I shouldn't question, want things I shouldn't want. Not even on purpose, they're good guys I know they want the best for me just like your friends do," Dawson paused to take a breath. He had this look on his face that was so blank it looked painful. His gaze was distant and fixated on nothing around him, but I felt like he could see a movie playing in his head.

"Things at home are weird for us, Jesse. Mom is always sad about dad cheating and leaving her, and she can't move on. She looks like she's barely trying but I know this is as hard as she can push herself. There's this void that I see everywhere I go and it reminds me about how brutal people can be and how weak we are. I can't do anything about this, or her, and I feel like I'm nothing sometimes," he continued. "Like I can't feel anything, every time I'm with people besides family, I feel like I'm missing out on something. Like I can't be as carefree as them, I can't look at myself and say, 'hey things are great'…"

"What does that have to do with not wanting to be around me? You said everyone besides, family, so talk to me more, include me because I don't make you feel that way and maybe I can make it stop," I said.

Dawson looked right at me, his face red from the blood rushing to his head after lying down on the cement ground for so long, and from the alcohol that was surprisingly starting to kick in even more. We were sitting three feet apart from each other, but I felt like his face was an inch away from mine. I didn't understand why Dawson's eyes were starting to wander, or why sweat was beading on his forehead. I didn't understand why this boy next to me seemed like everything my brother was not, yet it felt like this was the only side I should've known.

"These cement tiles, these gates, these four walls...you, mom... this familiarity...it's the only thing that makes me feel right, the only thing that makes me feel like I know who I am and that I don't need to use up all the strength I have to hold myself together," Dawson said slowly, calmly. "My friends worry about me a lot, I know they do. I don't want them to ask you questions that you can't answer, I don't want them to make you think that I'm not okay."

"You don't sound okay," I whispered.

"I need to know how to look at people living their lives without wondering why I can't look at life the way they do, and I need to do it on my own, without the familiarity." Dawson sat up abruptly, steadying himself with his palms pressed so tightly against the floor that I could see the flesh beneath his fingertips turning white.

The sun was almost completely visible now, but when I looked at Dawson it felt like the sky was still dark.

"I love this place, and I love you, but I can't feel anything about me."

CHAPTER 3

A SURPRISE

―

"I love this place, and I love you, but I can't feel anything about me."

I thought about that sentence a lot. The more I thought about, the sadder it sounded and the more it felt like a cry for help. I wondered why I wasn't so adamant on making Dawson open up about what he felt. He had all his walls up, he always had, but the fact that he had said that to me made me feel like I could've brought those walls down.

Saturdays were always the hardest days to deal with. Unlike most of the kids my age, looking forward to sleeping in and lazing around at home to celebrate the first day of the weekend, Saturdays made me extremely anxious. I hated the scent that would creep up through the crack at the bottom of my bedroom door. It was the smell of fresh flowers and strong perfume. It woke me up each time without fail. Saturdays this year left an even worse taste in my mouth just because I had to open my door to see Dawson's empty room staring at me from across the floor. His bed was made and there were stacks of clothes folded on it. The corners of some of his band posters were starting to peel off the wall. If he was here, he would be frantically searching around the house for tape or sticky tack to put them back into place.

The smell started to creep into my room a little after nine in the morning, after my mother came back from the market with random ingredients to stuff in the fridge and a large bouquet of daisies. It was a weekly routine. She always got so dressed up to go, putting on so much makeup and mixing together all the scents from her fragrances and body creams. She would also refuse to acknowledge the excessive amount of ingredients already living in the fridge.

"There still isn't enough to last the week," she would say every time I brought it up.

I wondered if she thought I was still a child, still gullible and ignorant. I wonder if she really assumed that I was unable to feel how her fingers were always shaking slightly when she cupped my face in her hands after I would come downstairs to greet her.

I was very little when my father walked out on us and I barely remember spending a single minute with him. But I do remember how going to the market each week was his idea. He was always talking about fresh fruits and vegetables and how he loved the feeling of waking up in the morning to feel the sense of community that came with shopping for groceries there. The market wasn't too far away from our house, probably a five minute walk. The market had rows of big yellow umbrellas shielding tables of fresh meat and produce from the sun. I hated going to the market because groceries don't excite me, but I could definitely see why my dad enjoyed it so much. For people like my parents, the market was their version of a giant college mixer. My mother was always just a tag-along, an observer as he picked out the vegetables and meats to cook lunch. My father was more of the chef in the household, always experimenting with different recipes and making new sauces to go with fried chicken or fish.

Dawson and I always hated how our mom kept going to the market every Saturday, even a decade after him leaving her. It made time in the house feel stagnant, like that big void that Dawson had told me about. Dawson had always explicitly expressed his discontent, throwing around occasional snarky comments that left pained expressions on her face.

"He's moved on. Probably doesn't even think about you or us anymore. You're really going to give him the satisfaction of having you wrapped around the idea of him by going on these stupid market runs?" Dawson once said as she left the house. He never looked away from the TV screen, his face blank as she clutched her knit bag a little tighter in her hand at the doorway.

"I'll see you in a bit, honey," she said that day with a smile as she walked out the door.

I came downstairs to see her wearing a light blue sundress with frills at the hem and three big black buttons down her chest. It fit her slender frame perfectly as it hung around her ankles, the soft fabric brushing against the bottom of the couch. She was wearing dark red lipstick that contrasted strongly against her pale face and dark hair. She looked beautiful as she always did. She looked like she was waiting for someone and I always felt that she dressed up hoping to bump into my father there one more time.

"Aren't they pretty in the sunlight?" she asked, her eyes fixed longingly on the crystalized pink vase that now housed a fresh bouquet of light yellow daisies. They looked like they were being baked golden under the honey-colored rays coming in from the window. She asked me the same question each and every week—the same intonation, the same desperate tinge of approval, the same tremble in her voice.

"They look beautiful, just like you," I said, sitting down next to her and giving her hand a little squeeze. I could never say the things Dawson would say to her. I couldn't even bear the thought of doing anything that would wipe the soft smile off her face.

"Thank you, honey," she said with a smile. Her smile made the room feel soft and warm, even more gold than the sun. "I got ingredients to make fish curry, it'll be done in an hour so we can have lunch together soon. You'll be having lunch here right?"

I nodded, happy that she was cooking something she really enjoyed making. Fish curry was a big specialty of hers, and it was well raved about at parties and potlucks. It was also Dawson's favorite thing to eat. I wondered if her cooking the dish made it feel like he was there with them, although he stopped eating lunch with us on the weekends, way before he ran away.

Lunch with my mother was a big part of my weekends and it was probably my favorite part. We would bring the food out to the living room and watch Korean dramas on TV. I found the greatest satisfaction watching her react to them—she would cry, laugh until she couldn't breathe and even throw swears at the screen. I liked seeing her show her emotions and she always gave the same old smile all the time that it was hard to tell what she really felt anymore.

After lunch, my mom headed up to her bedroom for an afternoon nap and I headed up to mine. My sheets were warm from being hit by direct rays of sunlight piercing through my window. I took my shirt off and lay on my bed, wriggling around to find a comfortable spot since the fabric felt itchy under my skin.

I stared at the ceiling fan above me, its squeaky creaking becoming a layer of calming white noise around the bedroom. I stared at the rotating blades and the perfect circle its movements made, counting softly under my breath in an attempt to calculate how many perfect rotations the blades could make in the brief silence between the sounds of two creaks. It felt like I was in physics class.

It was pointless. The blades were moving too fast for him to see what point would determine one complete rotation. It was as pointless as trying to throw a cotton ball over the fence onto his neighbor's car.

I kept hearing bits and pieces of that conversation with Dawson, it was so vividly etched into my memory that it felt like something from yesterday and not more than a week ago. I couldn't help but let the aching feeling in my chest grow. Was he feeling the same things now, wherever he was? Was he feeling good things, or bad? Did he have someone to depend on, or was he alone?

I was snapped out of my thoughts by a knock on the door.

"Can I come in?" The hushed question (or more so an attempt at being hushed) broke through the calm of my white noise.

I sat up to see Gryme's head peeking through the crack in the door, a cheesy grin on his face. It was hard not smile too.

"What are you doing here? It's 1:00 p.m. on a Saturday. You're supposed to be sleeping with a half-eaten burger on your belly," I said with a laugh as Gryme walked over and flopped himself on my bed like it was his own. His face twisted in discomfort as the bare skin on his arms made contact with the warm sheets.

"That definitely sounds much better than spending 1:00 p.m. on a Saturday staring at a ceiling fan on a bed that feels like the surface of the sun," Gryme said, peeling the sheets off one half of the bed and dropping the weight onto my legs. It was my turn to be uncomfortable now. "But no, I didn't head out to get a burger last night because I'm grounded," Gryme added.

"You're grounded. And you're here?"

"You're such a noble guy, Jesse, always so good. My mum's always loved you, wanna switch homes for a week?" Gryme got off the bed and started rummaging through my closet. I opened my mouth to say something, but I decided to shut up since it probably wouldn't have made much difference anyway.

"Shut up," I said, glaring at the bag in Gryme's hand. It was the one I used in my first year of high school. It had an obnoxiously large skeleton patch stitched messily right in the middle of it because I was going through a big heavy metal and grunge phase at the time. One day, the whole group sat me down in the field to tell me that as much as they loved me, the bright red flames piercing out of the skeleton's eyes were a bit much for even them to handle. They followed me to the mall that evening and helped me switch it out for a plain black Adidas backpack that looked much more socially acceptable.

Gryme grabbed a faded blue backpack lying on the bedroom floor and stuffed the first few t-shirts and hoodies he could grab off the closet rack into it. He laughed looking at it.

"What are you doing, Gry?"

He turned around, the skeleton backpack thrown over his shoulder as he stood proudly in his same old unwashed green hoodie. It still smelled like two-month-old barbecue sauce.

"We're going on a road trip, Jesse boy. Tell your mum we'll be back in a couple days."

"I can't do that."

"Actually, you don't have to, she already knows. Don't you just love a good term break? Now let's go!" Gryme grabbed the backpack and ran out the door. I stood in the middle of my room confused as ever, slowly picking up a couple more shirts and some pairs of underwear because he was pretty sure Gryme didn't stuff a single one into the bag. I realized that I didn't even know the term break started on Monday, and that made me uncomfortable considering how I would always count down to that. I must be really out of it.

I walked out of my room and made my way to my mom's door, ready to knock and wake her up from her nap if I had to. Right at that moment, the door swung open and she stood there, her face a little puffy from her sleep and her hair in messy knots on one side of her face.

"You must have had one heck of a sleep, mom," I said a little surprised, using my fingers to smoothen the knots out. She let out an airy laugh and held onto my hand.

"Have a safe trip, okay? Give me a call when you reach, and make sure Gryme doesn't drive too fast!" she said, her grip on my hand tightening at the end of her sentence. I couldn't blame her, Gryme makes all parents worry.

"Why did you even let me go? This is all too sudden, I really don't want to leave you alone but he's already in the car and…"

My mom took my face in both her hands and gave me a smile. It was a really warm one, the kind that made me feel like I was five years old again and never wanted her to let me go.

"You would have been sitting here in the house the whole term break if your friends didn't drag you out like this, I know just as much as they do," she said, using her thumb to caress my cheek. Her hands smelled like cherry blossom lotion, the same kind she's always been using ever since I was a baby. It was another one of her signature scents. "No more moping, Jess. I want you to know what it feels like to have the sun on your skin again. I want you to remember how much you love it and you've always loved adventure ever since you were little."

I didn't know what to say about the fact that my own mother was saying this to me. I thought I was concealing this whole teenage confusing thing from her pretty well. There was something about the way she was looking at me that made me feel a lump in my throat, and I forcefully swallowed my own saliva to try and knock the feeling away. I knew what she might have been thinking that she already watched one son walk away consumed by his thoughts, so maybe she was trying to help set me free from mine.

"I'll call you when I reach," I said, taking her hands in mine and giving them a kiss.

* * *

Gryme's trunk was filled with blankets and giant plastic bags of bread—it was a staple for us whenever we took trips out of town, which didn't really happen that often.

Gryme grabbed a sardine bun and headed to hop into the driver's seat. His car looked exactly like what somebody would expect from a teenage boy with a laundry pile that's at least five weeks old. I slid into the passenger seat, and I had to admit that I had missed the musky mixed smells of ash, leftover soda and his hanging pine-tree shaped air freshener that had a stronger scent of dried leaves than it did of a "forest breeze." It's definitely been a while since we went anywhere in this bad boy.

I hoped that Gryme would say anything at all about whatever this plan was supposed to be, but he simply lit a cigarette up, put an old CD in the car radio and backed out of the parking spot to hit the road. No conversation popped up at any point through the first few minutes of the ride, which was unusual despite the fact that I could almost feel him holding his breath to keep himself from saying anything he wasn't supposed to. Out of everything that was going on, nothing confused me more than the fact that the rest of my friends trusted Gryme (of all people) to stay silent and keep a secret.

"You remember that empty shop lot we used to go to in our first year of high school?" I asked, looking out the car window to take in a view that was far from scenic but close to his heart. Grey telephone poles covered with torn worn-out posters of ads selling furniture and Chinese psychic services. Kids racing on their bicycles with no shirt or shoes on but they were waving flip-flops around in their hands. A row of empty concrete lots that were once grocery stores, coffee shops, laundromats and rusty metal grills signaling their closure but their fraying signage at the front of the store still in place.

"How could anyone ever forget that good old hideout?" Gryme asked, his face stretched out into another one of his cheesy grins. "What made you think about it?"

"I've been thinking about it a lot these past few weeks, I don't know," I said, shrugging my shoulders. "It just keeps popping up in my mind. Maybe I need a hideout. Maybe that's why I'm so calm about how you're kidnapping me and not saying anything about it right now."

"We could be on the way to the least hideout place on the planet right now. What if I told you I'm taking you to the mall? Not one mall, but all the malls, and the bread's in the trunk so we don't have to spend any money on stupid mall food."

I turned the music up, shaking my head as Gryme looked over at me with wide eyes and raised eyebrows. I jabbed him in the shoulder.

Looking back over the years, I suppose that impromptu plans were our default way of snapping each other back to reality. After Kivo's parents moved to London for work without him two years ago, we dragged him out of Biology class to ditch school and climb a big palm tree behind an old bungalow a couple streets away. I remembered how Kivo broke the news to us, talking about how excited he was to be stuck with the driver and the maid every day in a big house with nobody to stop him from gaming all day. We all saw right through it though, we could literally hear him screaming "This house is too big for me to be comfortable alone and I don't know what to do with myself!"

"I want you to climb that palm tree and get that wrinkly grandpa-looking coconut up there, it looks like it was supposed to fall fifteen years ago," Mitchell said to a gaping Kivo, the five foot five baby-faced brunette, letting his eyes drift from the base of the trunk to the towering greens above him.

"Why would I do that?" I remembered how soft Kivo sounded, his timid frame rocking back-and-forth on his heels. Kivo had always been their little monkey since elementary school, using his small agile frame to his benefit by climbing walls and creating ridiculous parkour routines on car bonnets, apartment balconies or rooftops. We would always get so worried, taking any opportunity we could to scream and beg him to get his feet on anything not elevated off the ground. But he always looked so much happier when he was doing something crazy, something that made him move a little faster, reach a little higher. Kivo was a rich boy who grew up in one of the biggest houses in town, his bedroom was bigger than my living room and kitchen put together. But It was a big house with no space—no space to be daring, no space to be adventurous. There was only space to close deals and move forward, sign checks and make plans.

"I haven't seen your feet off the ground in a while man. Maybe with your parents gone, you can turn your room into a little skate park, we thought we'll give you a little challenge to practice with," I had told him.

"Jesse, this tree is fucking high, what if I fall or die?"

"The rooftop of Cassie's apartment was way higher, we died just looking at you," Mo chimed in. "No, wait, actually, how the hell did you even get up there?"

Looking back over the years, we always did the craziest things.

As Gryme switched the music in the car to an old album by The Strokes, the only thing I could see in my head was Kivo climbing up that tree. Pale skinny toes clamoring onto rough brown bark, movements so swift it seemed as if the tree had indentations ready for a tiny boy to fit his hands and feet for an easy climb.

I gazed out the window, looking at the blurry passing road signs signaling the fact that I was moving quickly further away from my house. With each passing minute, I felt like Kivo, swiftly climbing to the top, closer to the sky and further off the ground. I leaned my head on the glass and caught my reflection in the car's side mirror, a little surprised at how tired I actually looked with the dark shadows around my eyes and flaky skin on my unmoisturized cheeks after weeks of skipping out on my acne-prevention routine. I realized that I didn't know when the last time I looked at a mirror last to take a good look at myself. The last few days especially had passed by me in such a whirlwind despite the fact that I wasn't doing much, I could only remember the time I spent time awake through the amount of time I spent stuck thinking about the past.

The car drove past a large complex of cream-colored build-ings, but with all the cream stained by aging black smudges from the emerging cement and brick beneath the paint. It used to be a recreation house for British colonizers, equipped with a tennis court, a miniature soccer field, a pool (that was now filled with dried leaves and red ant nests) and even a gazebo structure that used to house a cocktail bar. The buildings were abandoned now, kept in its place for historical purposes to recognize the country's colonial era and the local individuals that worked in the estate tirelessly as the help of these foreigners. It was located on the edge of town, meaning that Gryme was definitely heading to cross the state border.

"All these malls you're taking me to must sure be great if we're leaving the state for them," I said, in a sing-song voice following the tune of the song blasting through the speakers.

Gryme merely laughed and let out a loud hush sound, using the tips of his fingers to squeeze his own lips shut.

In that moment, with my eyes fixed on the buildings slowly moving out of sight, I could see Kivo's face when he reached the very top of the tree. It was the brightest smile we had seen from him in a while, it was a visible weight lifted off his shoulders as he reached for the old coconut and threw it all the way to the ground, the fruit breaking into an explosion of pieces of dry husk landing on all their shows.

I felt like the clouds hanging over my head were getting a little less gray too.

CHAPTER 4

THE DESTINATION

————

The last time I took a trip out of town was a little over two years ago with Dawson and my mom. It was the first time the three of us had a vacation alone, we were usually joined by all my mom's siblings and their fleet of toddlers. The adults basically looked at Dawson and me as their nannies for the trip, as they left their kids with us while the rest of them went for drinks at bars around the area.

"Now this...this feels like a vacation," Dawson said, setting his bag down on the bed as he looked out the glass panels separating our hotel room from the balcony.

It was an amazing view. My mom had used up years' worth of points collected on her credit card to redeem a beach villa getaway a couple states up north. The ocean wasn't the kind of blue that you would see on postcards. Instead it was slightly cloudy and murky, taking on the hues of a more seaweed green. Despite the fact that I would probably opt out of snorkeling in it, I had to admit that it was beautiful. There were big green mountains surrounding our resort, housing tropical rainforests that were never free of the sounds of chirping birds, crickets and occasional monkeys screaming. Most of the room was decked out in modern Balinese wooden interior, the mix of dark and light shades of brown giving the space a certain depth that made it look so much bigger than it actually was. Everything smelled like the lemongrass and jasmine flowers with a tinge of ocean spray.

"Mom, how often do you even use your credit card? I'm getting kind of suspicious," I told her jokingly as I raised an eyebrow and peered into her hand bag.

My mom laughed and swatted my face away from her bag. "Don't say stupid things, I was just waiting for the right time to give us the time off we needed," she said, setting her bags down and sitting on the edge of the bed.

Dawson looked over at me with a small smile, nudging his head toward my mother to get me to look at her. They were playing the Hallmark channel on the TV and she had her eyes fixed on it, letting out a loud laugh as a group of friends on the screen broke out into a bar fight at somebody's wedding.

She had her feet tucked into fuzzy hotel slippers and she was tapping them on the ground to the beat of the background music in the show, and she grabbed a pillow from the bed and hugged it underneath her chin.

It was the first time in years that we had seen her that relaxed.

Dawson and I went to join her, wedging her between us as we sat on either side of her. I put my head on her shoulder while Dawson wrapped one of his arms around both of us.

"My big boys acting like babies again," she said, giving me a kiss on the top of my head and giving Dawson a kiss on the cheek.

"Thank you mom, we really did need this," Dawson said.

* * *

Thinking about the trip felt like I was dreaming. It felt like a time too far from now.

The road out of town wasn't as quiet as it usually was; there was a good amount of cars probably filled with families taking their kids for holidays over the term break. It made me think about my last family trip a whole lot—the laughs on our drive there and back, seeing my mom and brother's faces all day without an ounce of worry, being free of the void that ate us up when we were at home.

"Really though, how much longer is it going to take until we get to wherever it is we're going," I asked Gryme, turning over to look at him with his sunglasses on even though everything was pretty dim from all the trees surrounding both sides of us.

We had been on that same stretch leading up to the highway for almost two hours now, and the view outside the window had been exactly the same. There were just a lot of trees out here, I felt like I was stuck in a GIF. The fact that I had no indication on when this loop of trees was going to end made me restless and my habit of shaking my legs kicked in.

"That sounds annoying; stop doing that, Jesse," Gryme said, pinching the skin on my knee to get me to stop hitting it against the car dashboard.

"I'll stop if you tell me where we're going," I said in a teasing voice, keeping my gaze fixed ahead of me as I bit my lip to remain calm when Gryme pinched even harder. The calmness that I initially felt at the start of our drive was slowly wearing off and it was being replaced with a pulsing frustration. I tried to recognize the sights around me. I felt like I had been here before, and not just because it looked like any other highway leading out of the state. I somehow remembered the faded gray asphalt of the road feeling warm as it pressed against my back, and I remembered seeing the exact same red and white signs of a roadside stall selling rice and curry.

"We're almost there, anything ringing a bell?" Gryme asked me.

I slowly turned to look at him, he had a newly lit cigarette lightly perched between his lips and I had to pause for a second just to try to understand how he managed to pull that out in those few seconds that I looked away. So I wasn't wrong and imagining these familiar things I was feeling. Maybe I had been here before and probably with Gryme too.

The car turned into a narrow road that barely fit its entire width. Everything around us was just trees, bushes and abandoned wooden houses on stilts. The road kept going and Gryme kept driving, putting his head out the window to puff out clouds of smoke.

"I think I remember but I'm not sure what exactly I'm remembering," I said, my voice so low it was almost inaudible to myself. For some reason I felt nervous. It felt like the pit of my stomach was rising up to my chest. I didn't know how to explain it, but I felt like I was about to dig into an open wound. Why?

The car came to a stop, and Gryme yelled out a big, hearty "Hooray!"

I couldn't shake the feeling, I had my fingers gripping on the seat belt buckle while I stared blankly at the side mirror. A sharp slap on the back by Gryme's heavy arm jolted me right out of my trance.

"Hey," Gryme's smile was back, cheesy and widespread across his entire face. "Don't worry man, I'm not giving you up for a satanic ritual that involves your blood, you're with me, you don't have to look this scared."

For a split second, I noticed a slight shake at the corner of Gryme's lips. His bright expression fell to unveil fleeting undertones of worry and confusion.

"I'm not scared, man, shut up. I was just thinking about stuff," I said, unbuckling the seat belt and grabbing the cigarette out of his mouth for a quick puff.

"There you go, haven't seen you with that in a hot minute. You're always thinking about stuff, Jesse, and hopefully this helps," Gryme said as he got out of the car. "Now grab the bread; let's go."

Standing in front of the car with a bag of bread held firmly in my hands, I stared at the sandy path in front of me. I could see a building peeking out between the leaves of the bush that we were parked behind. The walls were light brown, the doors and windows a shining white that I suspected was freshly painted. There were people laid out on deck chairs on the grassy lawns by the buildings front entrance. Black and gold letters perched on the roof read out the words "Happy Holiday Inn."

It was all coming back to me.

"Happy Holiday Inn…" I whispered mouth agape. I was in shock at the fact that I didn't remember the road up to this place. Gryme ran to stand with his face right in front of mine. He had the most excited doe-eyed expression on his face.

"Remember our first big boy trip, Jesse? And I guess big girl trip too if you wanna count Cassie as anything else other than a mean dude," Gryme said, pushing his Ray Bans down onto the tip of his nose. "Well, we figured that you might want more honesty hours and self-exploration missions with your best friends. It's been a while, man."

I smiled and I felt the smile spread all across my whole body, a slow warmth building up in my chest, my stomach, my fingertips and even my toes. "I remember that trip. Well some parts of it at least, the ones my brain could hold," I added with a laugh. I guess I was just thinking that this was going to be something bad, my mind really plays tricks on me sometimes, making me doubt things I shouldn't be doubting. I wondered if all the distance I was putting between myself and those around me was just a product of my own inability to differentiate fact from fiction.

"We were always thinking about going again, and we were so excited to just pack up and leave after finals but then Dawson left last year and well...we realize how hard it's been to get through to you since that day," Gryme said.

I looked down at my feet, biting my lips as I tried to think of a response. I turned to Gryme, opening my mouth to start saying something, but a flying finger was soon pressed against my lips to shut me up.

"Save your story time for when we actually walk in and meet everyone, because they've been texting me like crazy the past two hours because I was supposed to get to your place way before I actually did," Gryme said, pulling another pair of Ray Bans from his pocket and gently placing them on the bridge of my nose.

Gryme having an extra pair of sunglasses in his pocket was completely normal. On the other hand, the fact that the rest of them had trusted him, of all people, to drive me here on time on a Saturday afternoon—now that made no sense to me. I looked over to the car to catch him pulling out a half open can of Pepsi from the back seat to wash down an entire sardine bun that he had just chowed down in those few seconds after handing me the sunglasses.

"They wanted you to be on time, you? I asked.

"I didn't want to be in this situation either but they all got here in Mitch's mom's car and apparently, for some weird reason, I'm not allowed to be in it after that whole burger and beer situation of mine in the backseat," Gryme said.

I nodded, fully understanding the situation now. Gryme was drunk and left a half-eaten Quarter Pounder on Mrs. Tam's leather seats before spilling an entire bottle of beer all over the place, and on the burger. He still ate the burger though.

"Now, let's try to debunk that big old head of yours, Jesse boy."

We nodded to each other, bread and backpacks thrown over our shoulders, and made our way into Happy Holiday Inn.

* * *

The first time we came across the inn was through a simple Internet search for "cheap hotels in nature." Happy Holiday Inn had decent ratings, 3 stars out of 5 on average. The reviews said it was the perfect spot for backpackers that wanted to experience the rustic influences of British colonialism on present Southeast Asian architecture. The bedrooms and bathrooms weren't spotlessly clean, but they were decent enough to let us sleep on soft pillows and shower on floors with washed tiles and no odor.

The rooms were organized like a dormitory, with bunk bed rooms on one side of the inn while the other side had rooms with six to eight beds lined up in a row. The price was perfect for a bunch of high school kids whose only savings came up from not using our monthly allowance on food and games. It was the perfect atmosphere for kids who weren't dirt rich (with the exception of Kivo) but who were also well off enough to live comfortably and enjoy holidays around neighboring states or countries.

The inn was about a two to three hour drive from town, and it stood deep in an inner road leading up to a row of mountains that were big tourist attractions for those who came from Europe or America. We had booked our first three-night stay here after ten minutes of deliberation.

"It looks and smells exactly like I remember," I said, dropping my bags by my feet in the lobby. There were foreigners roaming around all over the place. Tall white girls were still clad in only bikinis and sun hats as they walked out on the lawn, even though it barely felt like sun tanning weather to me. In fact, for the locals, it was a moderately gloomy day.

"We came here last June, not 10 years ago, how much did you expect it to change," Gryme's voice trailed off as his eyes followed a tan Southern American looking girl in a tight mustard sundress walking past him. "It definitely looks exactly like I remember with hotties everywhere. Hotties that I have zero chance with unless they like it chubby in Brazil," he added.

"About damn time you idiots!"

We jumped at the shrill voice projected right at us, a shrill voice that could only belong to Cassie.

Cassie had her dark hair pulled back into two little space buns at the side of her head, her hazel skin exposed in a pair of denim shorts and a white tube top. She stormed up to us, the sound of her flip-flops slapping loudly on the lobby's wooden floor.

"No beating people up in public, Taz. At least they're here now," Mitchel trailed behind her, picking up his pace to put an arm around her waist and pull her a few steps back. Gryme and I looked at each other, eyebrows slightly raised. When did Mitchel get to touch Cassie without a slap in the face?

Mo and Kivo stood behind them, catching our eye as we looked over to Mitch and Cassie and back at them. The two boys only shrugged and clamped their mouths shut to avoid a smile. Gryme nudged me hard and I nudged back. We were definitely going to have a fun time looking into things throughout our stay.

"So I may have reached Jesse's house a teeny tiny bit later than usual because I may or may not have woken up a teeny tiny bit later after you guys left to get here," Gryme said, holding the bag of bread in front of him as Kivo and Mo walked up to us. I had to bite onto my lip to keep from laughing when I noticed the look on their faces seeing Mitchel's fingers lightly wrapped around Cassie's wrist. It was their turn now to look over at us with the same raised eyebrows that Gryme and I had given them.

"We'll get to the bottom of this, boys," Mo whispered.

Mitchel grabbed a chicken floss pastry from the bag before putting his hands on my shoulders and pushing me toward the lobby elevator. The rest of the group trailed behind, muffled complaints and slaps on the arm, the only thing audible to anybody that walked past us. "We managed to get the same room we got the last time we came here, six beds, one bathroom, a complete mess but this time we brought more trash bags and more….fun surprises."

The elevator was tiny, and the six of us tried to make ourselves fit comfortably by forming a tight little circle. I looked
around, looking at each of everyone's faces as they laughed,
chatted and showed each other memes on their phones. I
could hear the creaking of the old elevator as it made its way
up to the fourth floor, and the only thing I could think about
was how great it was to be able to be caught in questionable
situations with the people surrounding me right now.

"So, does anybody want to tell me what we're doing here this
weekend? And why did I have to be left out of planning this
thing? If you guys were pissed at me because of how I acted
at the beach then…"

Mo cut me off. "Chill out, dude, of course we're not mad. Now
stop rambling or you're going to ruin the surprise."

The elevator bell rang and we were at the fourth floor. The
door opened up to the smell of cigarette smoke, flavored
vape juices and whiskey, laced together with the fresh feel
of forest breeze on their skin. The fourth floor was made of
long open corridors that let you look out over the ledge into
the trees and the lawn up front.

"Smells like teen spirit right here," Mo said with a laugh,
before nudging me out of the elevator. "Our room's at the
very end of the corridor."

I remembered things feeling different a year ago when we came here. We had all cramped up into Kivo's mum's min-ivan together and pulled up in the inn's parking lot for an hour to pass around a bottle of vodka. By the time we had reached the fourth floor, we were a messy human pile of giggles, blurry vision and toppled-over bags.

I didn't think I was in the right state of mind at the time to really look at how everything looked around me. I didn't take the time to process how I really felt, and as much as I loved living in the moment, everything around me was moving too fast at the time for me to savor any of those moments and appreciate them. Right now, I could see everything as it really was. I could see my friends walking in front of me as we walked down the corridor together, surrounded by deep rich greenery. The sound of our voices sprinkled in the air with the chirping of birds and a mix of different languages from the backpackers on the ground floor of the inn.

This is my life, unapologetically free, beautiful and up to my own interpretation. I wondered how many other kids my age wished they could have people that knew them like the back of their hands. I wondered how many other kids my age wished they could be in this inn right now in what felt like the middle of nowhere, with the complete independence to have fun and find the answers they were looking for. It was this lingering sense of appreciation that made my mind a mess. I had no reason to be alone when I had so many hands reaching out for me to hold. Even with all that, I still felt like I was being suspended over a life that I had no control over, a life where I was trapped by discontent that I shouldn't even be feeling.

"Close your eyes, Jesse," Gryme said.

We were standing right in front of Room 425, the smell of paint reaffirming my assumptions that all the white doors and windows were indeed freshly painted.

"Well, you're taking too long so I'm gonna just cover your eyes for you, open the door, Kiv!"

Gryme slapped his hands onto my face, and I let out a pained grunt. His hands had rough patches of skin from lifting weights at the gym, and all I wanted to do was make sure there weren't any calluses scratching my eyelids.

"Surprise, Jesse boy."

When Gryme lifted his hands off, I needed a quick second to readjust my sight to the bright colors bouncing off the graffiti walls inside the room and the sunlight beating into it. I squeezed my eyes together and then opened them again.

This time, I noticed a shadow by the doorway, a shadow that was getting bigger as though it was walking toward me.

"Wait." I felt my breath hitch in my throat. There was the same nervous feeling I felt in the car weighing down on my chest. It felt like I was about to dig into an open wound. The shadow approaching the doorway looked like it was moving in slow motion. All of my friends had their faces twisted into something that was a cross of eagerness and anxiousness. It looked like time was moving a few beats slower than it usually did.

Then, I felt my breathing stop.

I recognized that shadow. The broad shoulders and tall frame, "Wait, what do you mean?" I said again, unable to continue.

Standing in the doorway was Dawson Loo, looking just as sculpted and dashing as ever in a plain white t-Shirt and basketball shorts, his face bearing the same boyish features that were now even more defined because of his shorter hair. I stood frozen, my fingers gripping tightly at the sides of my sweats.

"Your arms are looking a little smaller there, little bro."

CHAPTER 5

QUESTIONING

—

The morning after Dawson left home was the hardest morning I had to wake up to. I opened my eyes, my ears tuning in to the familiar sound of my creaking ceiling fan. I still slept with a blanket on that night even though it was practically burning in my room. I wanted to feel the weight of it on me, the pressure on my skin made me feel safe and protected. I didn't get much sleep and I probably drifted off a little after the sun came up. I had to keep a pillow on my face all night to help me muffle out the noise of my mom crying in her room next door. When Dawson walked out the gates, the two of us waited by the front door, hoping that the longer we stared at his back walking away from us, the more we could help him realize that he was making a mistake. The sound of his car leaving the driveway and down the street was all she needed to shut herself in her room the whole night. I had spent hours knocking slowly on her door, asking every few minutes if she needed a glass of water, a snack or a walk. Each time, I would hear a sniffle.

"I'm good Jesse, just give me a little more time," she would say faintly.

Each time, I could hear the usual smile she had in her warm voice. I could also hear the strain in her throat from making it sound that way. I didn't understand why she wanted to hide it when she had nothing to be ashamed of. She was rightfully angry and rightfully devastated. She had gone through enough with my dad walking out on us and now Dawson was doing the same thing.

"I love this place, and I love you, but I can't feel anything about me."

The night Dawson left, that line was the only thing I could hear. I heard it when I came home to him in the living room, sitting down on the couch with his face buried in his hands and his elbows propped up on shaking knees. He looked around almost frantically when he heard the sound of the front door closing, his eyes wide when he saw me standing there frozen as I tried to take in what I was seeing. There were two large duffel bags on the floor and they looked completely filled. Dawson's face was a pale white, his pupils darker than usual and the white in his eyes were tinted with a slight red that I could notice even from five feet away. There were bags under his eyes and the veins on his eyelids were more obvious than usual.

"What's going on?" I asked him. I remember feeling like I was about to step onto a floor full of broken glass.

"I can't be here anymore," he said, staring right at me.

Waking up the morning after that was the hardest thing I had to do. Opening my room door and stepping outside would make everything real. The Dawson I saw that night wasn't the brother I grew up with, he was the brother that I was introduced to at six in the morning in the middle of August as I lay down drunk on my front porch. It was a brother that was broken.

But I didn't do anything to fix him.

"Do you think he stole the car?" my mom had asked me quietly, after finally deciding to get out of her room the next afternoon for a cup of hot milk with me in the kitchen.

"We both know Dawson's not like that." I really meant that. He didn't care too much about school, and yes he skipped class to shoot hoops or smoke himself out in an alley, but he would never do any sort of crime. I heard that line again.

"I feel like I did something wrong. Did I not care enough? I've always tried to be both parents for the two of you, but maybe stepping back to start dating again was the worst thing I could have possibly done."

"Mom, no, that's not it. Dawson's the one that convinced me to be fine with you dating; he always supported you and everything you did. You did nothing wrong." I didn't know how to explain to her what Dawson was feeling. Sometimes words just weren't enough to tell a whole story. She had to notice the little things—the way his eyes would dart around uncomfortably when he stepped into a room full of people, the way he had just started fidgeting with his fingers when he wasn't doing anything in particular or just the fact that he could no longer stay at home to watch TV or play video games all day. These were little things that a person could just credit to just growing up and feeling more restless with the idea of themselves, a strong urge to get out there and find something new that could stimulate the senses. But after talking to Dawson that night, I realized that there could be a whole lot more to the story.

The changes in his attitude were too drastic. The things that he used to find enjoyment in looked like they were suffocating him. He had to move about, so he did, he was always out with friends, playing soccer or just driving around looking for things that he could help out with around town for a small amount of money. Productivity and distraction are two very distinct things, separated by the intention one has in mind. They both keep you busy, and they both tire you out, but only one gives you genuine satisfaction, an inkling of a smile at the end of the day to celebrate a task being complete. Distractions don't do that. Distractions create a different form of exhaustion, one that stems from running around with no exact direction. Distractions are driven by feelings, mostly by the fear of them.

I think my brother was scared of something.

* * *

I was looking at Dawson standing in front of me, in person, after more than a year of not hearing his voice or hearing anything at all about where he might have been. It was a little too much for me to handle. I felt like my head was spinning and my legs were getting wobbly. I wanted to bolt right out of there to find a place where I could just sit and think and piece together all the questions in my head. I had so many questions but I needed to find somewhere to even begin asking. But I couldn't move, my feet felt like they were stuck on the floor, like they were held down by weights that made it impossible for me to lift them off the tiles.

"Jesse, I know this is weird and you have every reason in the world to be mad at us for not telling you sooner and dragging you out here like this…" Cassie said, slowly walking up to me.

"It was my idea, I told them not to say anything," Dawson interrupted her.

I slowly backed away, pausing to take a breath before I spoke. "I'm going to get some air, I'll be right back."

Walking away from the room and heading down the corridor felt a lot like how I felt walking away from them at the beach. I didn't know where exactly I wanted to go, but I just needed to feel like I was getting further away from something. Nobody was chasing me this time, and I couldn't hear faint footsteps in the background. But I still felt a looming shadow right behind me, looking over my shoulder. It was like there was another version of myself clinging onto my back like a child, begging me to run away with him on my back. I went back into the elevator and hit the button to head back to the ground floor. I didn't know what was going through my mind, but it was a lot of things. It was a mixture of joy, anger and fear, joy from finally seeing my brother again, anger from the fact that I was so close to where he was without me even knowing, and fear that I was going to have go through another goodbye when I really wasn't in the right place for one right now.

"What am I doing?" I muttered under my breath. I had my eyes locked to the ground, watching my beat up sneakers take frantic steps.

It was a terrible feeling, the kind that made you see nothing when you looked out ahead of you. I've always had them, these little episodes where I suddenly felt like I wasn't in this world, I wasn't in my world. Instead, I was living in a distorted version of it that was born out of most forgotten corners of my mind, the corners that lied to me and refused to let me acknowledge the world as it is. I call them episodes because they don't last very long, but they just keep coming.

In these episodes, I tend to feel myself falling. The scenes surrounding me tumble into a puddle of colors, scents and sounds. I can't distinguish much about what's unfolding but I can distinguish how out of place I am, and how far away I am from where I actually need to be.

I ran my fingers through my hair, pulling a little roughly on my short wavy locks in hopes that it would drag me out of this wormhole I felt I was in. I felt stupid every time I had an "episode." I felt weak for letting myself reach a place that almost sounded like I was almost pathologically crazy. I hated how I found myself in this place just because I had stumbled across something that made me think too much, if that made any sense.

I walked past the reception table in the lobby and stopped in my tracks to look around. I was in the middle of a bustling room and there were probably about fifty people in here. Some were rushing around with their luggage bags, some were still clad in their swimsuits even though the sun was starting to go down soon, some moved in obnoxiously loud groups of tourists yelling out their plans to explore a fishing village nearby to get a taste of authentic local food. It was a jumble of chaos and excitement, and for a second, I felt my head come back down from the clouds. I wanted to be a part of this scene unfolding before my eyes, it was normal. I wanted things to be normal.

"They just laid out more deck chairs in the lawn for people to see the sunset, man," a voice crept up behind me, getting increasingly loud. I turned around and saw someone walking up to me, a huge smile plastered on his face. He was a young boy and he didn't look anything more than a couple years older than me. He looked around Dawson's age actually, with the same lean and muscular built and the same kind of child-like features resting on sharp cheekbones and a chiseled jawline. He had a black t-shirt on with the words "Happy Holiday Inn" printed right down the middle, and he had a half-folded apron tied around his waist. I figured that he probably worked here.

"That sounds pretty cool, thanks," I said. "You work here?"

"Yeah, the inn just opened this cafeteria thing over there," the boy said, pointing across the lawn to a large wooden and glass structure that resembled something like a big open patio. It was pretty and full of people. I could see tables with stacks of plates on them from a distance.

"I got a job there a couple months ago as a kitchen boy, so if you want to know what's going on around here this weekend I'm a good person to check in with," he added with a laugh.

"That's awesome, that's exactly what my friends and I would need," I said, the words rolling off my tongue a little slowly. This conversation came so suddenly I was struggling to even find the words to say. I hope he didn't notice how much of disarray I was in.

"Anytime, my name's Tony," he said, reaching a hand out.

"My name's Jesse," I answered, shaking his hand firmly. I was trying my best to hold a tight smile on my face, but I noticed how his eyebrows raise right away and I figured that I must have looked like a complete idiot.

"You're Jesse?" he asked, still gripping my hand.

I cleared my throat, now completely confused. "You know me?"

* * *

Back at the room, they were all frozen in place. They expected Jesse to react the way he did, and they were prepared to see him walk away without saying anything. But now that it actually happened, they suddenly forgot how they were supposed to ease him through this.

"Let's just give him a while, I'll look for him in a bit and talk to him," Dawson said.

Dawson looked out over the ledge in front of their room and saw Jesse walking onto the lawn, sitting on one of the empty deck chairs. His elbows were propped up on his knees, his hands cupping both sides of his face. It was what Jesse always did whenever he needed to organize his thoughts. Dawson would always see him do that in his bedroom when he was studying for a test, in the living room when he was planning to break up with a girl and in the kitchen over cup noodles whenever his mom left to go out on a date with a new guy.

"You just pack all your stuff the night before, come home from school and tell mom at the dinner table that you're leaving home, with no explanation on where you're going, why you're going. Are you crazy?"

Dawson remembered how he had got about twenty voice-mails like those from Jesse the night he left. He listened to them all night, blasting them through the Bluetooth speakers in his car. He spent a lot of time contemplating the reasons why he should turn his car around and go home, hug his mom and Jesse and tell them he was sorry. The more he thought about it, the more obvious it was that there was more to gain than to lose if he ditched this whole escape plan of his. The benefits probably stood at a ratio of 100:1 next to the losses.

There was only one reason that drove him to do what he did, and somehow the weight of that just seemed too heavy to ignore:

He had to leave because his head was just…not where it needed to be.

CHAPTER 6

A SECOND FACE

The lobby started to drown out with the sound of muffled music blaring through speakers mounted on each of the room's four large walls. The speakers looked old and the scratched up sounds of bass strings booming through the room proved it.

"How'd you know my name?" I asked again. The boy named Tony looked slightly taken aback by the question. I noticed how he was shuffling his feet from side to side while he looked upward at the ceiling, looking as though he was trying to come up with a response.

"I know Dawson," he said after a few seconds, a shy smile spreading across his face. "He talks about you a lot."

"That's nice to hear," I replied, the words barely escaping my pursed lips as a murmur. Hearing Dawson's name again reminded me of the fact that I was standing right where I was, confused in an inn out of state, that I haven't been to in years. There were so many unanswered questions that I couldn't just let slide simply because I was too happy to see him again. Dawson left home after graduating high school without a word—no explanation, no information, no follow-up about his whereabouts. I couldn't understand why my friends thought that this was going to be a gracious reunion and something that I would accept with my whole heart.

Dawson was the only rock I had in a household that refused to recognize pain that needed to be recognized. He helped me realize that things at home were not healthy, that stifled conversations were pushing my mother deeper into a downward spiral, that it was forcing us to get used to the idea of letting the ghosts of our pasts dictate how we live our future. He opened a can of worms and then left, leaving me to deal with the consequences of the things that I now knew. He left without showing me how to hold things together without him. He left so silently that all this while I had almost made peace with the fact that he might be dead.

"I'm sure you have a lot of questions, you probably saw Dawson a little while ago," Tony continued. I kept my eyes locked on his, searching for any sort of sign that might show me how close he really was to Dawson. His eyes were soft, understanding, as though he felt the pain I felt and the way my brother had caused it. "I'm going to get back to work, hurry and head out to the lawn!"

Tony turned around. I watched his back as he walked away and I couldn't help but notice how he was built a lot like Dawson. Even their mannerisms were a little similar. I was unsure about how to process our conversation, but I decided to listen to what he said about the sunset.

I walked onto the lawn and like Tony said, there were more deck chairs spread out across the grass. People were laying down on them, huddled into small circles of family or friends. There were picnic mats spread out in the empty spaces between the chairs. Some of the mats had food on them and some of them were playing spaces for little kids. The sky was getting darker and everything fell more and more silent. I found the growing quietness pretty weird. I always assumed that when the night started to approach at a place like this, it would be greeted with more noise and vigor. I looked around and saw people stretched out on their chairs in hushed conversation and gentle laughter. It was an interesting observation. Everyone seemed like they were giving the sun its space to set, respecting its wishes to rest by keeping the surroundings soft.

I didn't know how long I had spent out on that deck chair. When I was done looking around and shifted my gaze ahead of me it was already almost pitch black. I didn't know what time it was and I didn't mind.

Then there were two little taps on my shoulder.

"Hey," a voice deep and familiar said. It was Dawson. I felt the weight shift at the edge of the chair and finally decided to stop staring at my feet and turn around. He looked nervous and it was a weird look on him. His shoulders were hunched forward and he was biting his lip, clearly unsure on how to start the conversation.

"So..." Dawson said slowly. "I don't even know where to begin but I'll answer anything."

"How about I not ask any questions and you tell me what's been going on?" I didn't intend to sound as angry as I did, and I was honestly surprised hearing how my voice raised once those words left my mouth.

Dawson's eyes widened, his fingers clasping his knees even tighter as he sat up straight. "I've been working here."

"Here, at this inn?"

"I wasn't intending to. After I left the house, I didn't know where to go," Dawson paused, shifting off the edge of the chair to face me a little more directly. "I heard you met Tony, I ran into him at the lobby and he told me that you were out here."

"Are you really going to just skip the whole part about running away and not knowing where to go and tell me about Tony and how you both work here?" My whole body was practically leaning forward at this point and Dawson looked growingly uncomfortable. I hoped that it would make him talk. "What happened to you? The last time I saw you was almost a year ago and you were barely recognizable to me but I still let you say nothing, hoping that you'd tell me soon enough."

Dawson's face fell, a mix between looking offended and disappointed that he had made his own brother doubt so much about him.

"But you didn't say shit to me, you just left." He used the tip of his index finger to lightly push me back a few comfortable inches away from his face. I was growing more and more frustrated at this point. "Get your hands off me," I said, pushing him back.

"I've been working at the front desk of a graphic design firm for the past year and a half. I noticed them hosting one of my friend's open mic events and I got to speak to one of the managers. I knew mom didn't like us working while we studied, but we both know that my grades aren't going to get any better even if I spend all my hours in a day looking at books."

"I know you're not stupid, Dawson."

"And I know I'm not too! Or at least, now I do," Dawson took a deep breath and let out a sigh. "I really liked my job. I worked the front desk but I also got to learn how to design, and I talked to all these clients that were coming in. They liked me and my work and they were just introducing me to all these different people. I realized that they knew so much more about the world than I did and they had seen so much more of the world than I did."

I blinked slowly. It was the first time that I had ever heard about Dawson having this job. I always assumed that he was out playing basketball or getting high with his friends.

"Wow, that sounds great," I meant what I said. Dawson having a job was a big deal, but it was a secret that I didn't understand why he had to go such lengths to keep. "But leaving home after graduating without telling your family, was the best way you could have done that?"

"I know that I could have handled everything a lot better, but I don't know, it really felt like there was no other way," Dawson got up and started pacing in front of the deck chair, his sandals making a rough scratch against the fake grass of the lawn. "I didn't know how to tell mom any of this and I didn't want to take no for an answer. Dad had always wanted me to be this successful person to carry on the family name, always hoping that one day I was going to surprise him with straight A's and show the world how smart I am. After he left, I didn't want mom to hold the same hope and be disappointed."

I was silent as I watched Dawson stop pacing. He was staring blankly at the gates of the inn. I also noticed the inn's emblem threaded on the back pocket of his shorts.

I felt like I hadn't thought about my dad as an actual person in years. He was always just this shadow that loomed around the house. Even though Dawson was only two years older than me, it felt as though those two extra years with our dad was all Dawson needed to build a relationship with a much stronger foundation than the relationship I had with him. The same sick feeling at the bottom of my stomach started to pool up. This time it was guilt, guilt for not missing my dad that way or not thinking about him as anything else, other than an inconvenience for my life, guilt for not realizing how a relationship with our father played into my brother's life and guilt for not trying to build a relationship in the first place. There was a part of me that insisted that my dad and I were just two different kinds of people that could never form the kind of love I wanted. But was it really okay for a child to think that way about a parent?

"I took the bus and got off at the rice and curry stall out on the main road for a really late dinner. I'm sure you remember seeing it on the way here you always talked so much about it. Then I saw the sign to this place," Dawson said, his hands were now on his hips as he looked right at me. "There were some backpackers eating at the table next to me and they were telling me about what a cool place it was, and then I realized the name was so familiar because you had told me about that trip you took here before."

I was listening so intently that I didn't realize how much louder everything was now. The sun had long gone into its rest, and everyone was done staying silent. There was music blasting through little speakers on the picnic mats. Pretty girls were dancing, showing off their very obvious tan lines. It had been a long time since I last had a long conversation with Dawson, the kind that made me lose all track of time. The last time it happened was that night I first sensed that something was off with him. I couldn't help but wonder that if I had taken that conversation a little more seriously, maybe I would have been able to help Dawson instead of letting him go through everything alone. I didn't want to repeat the same mistake.

"I went to the inn and I had no money to get a room so I decided to kill time by talking to the owner, he's a really chill guy who's always hanging around the bar after the inn clears up and everyone's pretty much asleep. Somehow we ended up talking about my situation, my interests and he offered me a deal to let me stay here if I could help him out with marketing and designing stuff."

"I thought you wanted to travel the world before college or something like that? I guess I'm trying to understand. What was it about this deal that made it sound like a better offer than being at home and saving up to do all the plans you wanted?" I asked.

"I got to use actual skills that I had learned from my job, in a place that was introducing me to people from all over the world, who were telling me stories and answering my questions. I told the owner that I would try it out for a little while, but the longer I stayed the more I realized how much I was learning. The money and the room isn't a bad thing to have either."

I smiled a little, a genuine response to what I was hearing. Dawson sounded passionate, and he sounded more sure of himself than he usually was. I took a deep breath and tried to ignore the fact that he really didn't answer my question all too much. He didn't explain much about the how's and why's.

He didn't tell me about Tony. In all honesty, there were a lot of missing links to his story. A brief image of his bloodshot eyes the night he left home flashed through my head.

But when I looked at him now, he seemed at peace. He was happier. I decided that I would ask him about it tomorrow, and try to savor this moment with a brother that I really missed.

"What are you smiling about?"

"It's just, such a 'you' thing to do. I don't agree with it, but it's brave and it's passionate, it's prioritizing solutions that are going to help you be a better person. You may have been bad at school but you were always good at improving yourself at everything else."

Dawson smiled too, sitting down right next to me. He put an arm around my shoulder cautiously, as if he was almost expecting me to swat it away.

"Thanks. I know there's still a ton more questions that need to be answered, but I feel bad for making your friends wait up in that room for hours. We have the whole weekend to piece things together."

There really was a lot to piece together. Dawson got up, signaling me to follow him toward the lobby. Lights on the lawn were now lit up, and it looked like an entire movie scene unfolding behind him; laughter, nature, families and friends. This was a setting that was completely out of my usual routine. It wasn't a regular Saturday night.

My brother had a smile on his face and it was a smile I reciprocated as I followed him through the crowd. But I couldn't keep the anxiousness from pooling in my throat. I knew that there was still something he wasn't telling me.

I'll think about it tomorrow.

CHAPTER 7

BUILDING BLOCKS

———

"Is it lonely for you, with just me here?" I had asked my mom one day. It was a quiet Saturday afternoon, and we were both curled up on either side of the couch after lunch. She was watching one of her favorite TV shows at the moment. It was a melodramatic Korean series about a woman who was struggling to find a job after being a housewife for so many years. Her life was completely flipped over after her husband had an affair and decided to walk out on her and both their kids. His business was failing and their kids were in pricey boarding schools.

Her eyes were fixed so intently on the scene unfolding before us. The woman had no money for a new place to live, so she was staying in her old house that was on an eviction notice. She went to sleep in a sleeping bag and she was always alone. There was no electricity in the house and there was no hot water, even though it was a cold winter in Seoul. It was a pretty shit position to be in. I wondered what was going through that woman's mind. How would it feel to wake up one day and find your life down a completely different path than what it was yesterday? How would you brace yourself for that uncertainty?

Was that how it was for my mom? She had to go through that twice, first with her husband and then with her son.

"Why would you ever say anything like that?" My mom replied, taking a little while to peel her eyes off the screen before she turned to face me. "Is everything okay?"

The worry in her voice frustrated me. I didn't understand how she could be worrying about me at this point when she was the one who was going through so much. All I wanted to do was take care of her. But how could I if I was letting every little thing stand in the way of me being strong and happy, everything I should be for her?

"I'm going to give you everything you deserve one day, mom. You don't have to worry about anything and you don't have to ever be alone. I'll never leave you," I said. I wasn't sure why I felt the need to say all of those things just then. Maybe it was me wondering if the reason she loved this show so much was because she could relate to the woman struggling in it. Maybe it was just prompted by how I was looking at her on the other side of this couch, her hair in a messy bun after cooking a big lunch for just the two of us. Suddenly, she looked so much older than I remembered. I didn't want her to age in pain.

My mom looked at me, her eyes soft and glistening. She took both my hands in hers. I felt the rough patches on her palm, probably from all the cooking and cleaning. She had chipped fingernails from biting them so much. I used to always make fun of her for that, but she would always tell me that working at an accounting firm forty hours a week was so dreadful sometimes that it gave her no choice.

"You're a young boy spending his Saturday afternoon watching sappy TV shows with his old mother. You've been giving me more than I could ever want," she said, bringing her hand up to my face and stroking my cheek gently. "All a mother wants is for her son to take care of himself. Can you do that for me?"

She left me speechless.

* * *

"Where are we going?" I asked Dawson as he led me through the crowd. We walked past a mother and her two sons. I couldn't tell their ages besides the fact that they both looked between the ages of three and five. The smaller boy was running up to his mom with a dried leaf he had found by his shoes. He gave his mother the leaf as a gift, a bright smile spreading into a stream of giggles as his mother held it to her heart and told him that she would keep it with her always.

It made me think about my mom. It made me think about the selflessness that she had when it came to us. Her gift was me even saying that I wanted to give her the world. She didn't really want me to though she wanted me to put all my energy into giving myself the world. She just wanted me to think of her, to hold her close to my heart and never let go. I watched Dawson's back as he made his way through all the people. I wanted to ask him if he ever thought about her. Did he ever think about how all this made her feel? I was happy for him a few minutes ago, but now I was just frustrated all over again. I took deep breaths, reminding myself that I would ask him later.

"I want you to meet someone. He's been taking care of me very well while I've been out here," Dawson said.

We walked up to a man sitting by the bar with a bottle of beer in one hand and a cigarette in the other. He was a burly man that looked like he was in his mid-forty's. His dark tanned skin gave off the impression that he spent a lot of his life traveling, probably the kind of traveling that involved many beaches, boats, mountains and caves. He kept his graying hair in a neat buzz cut and it made him look much younger in his cream-colored button-down shirt and khaki shorts.

It was dinner time, so the inn was still busy with people. The owner, who Dawson said introduced himself as Mr. Chip, was talking to a group of young German boys who looked like they were getting drunker by the second. Mr. Chips' face didn't show an ounce of discomfort though. Instead, it had the most genuine smile, one reminiscent of a father looking at a son. I wondered if my dad ever looked at us that way when we were growing up. Mr. Chip was asking the bartender for three glasses of warm water when we went to stand next to him.

"Hey, Mr. Chip," Dawson said, giving the man a light tap on the shoulder. Mr. Chip let out an excited grunt, getting off the bar stool to give him a hug. I looked at his face and how effortlessly happy he was when he got the hug.

"This is my brother, Jesse. He's staying here for the weekend with his friends."

"Hi, Mr. Chip," I reached my hand out for a handshake but was caught by surprise when he pulled me into a hug too. Mr. Chip smelled like expensive cologne, and his button-down was soft cotton that felt smooth and cold against the skin of his cheek. The embrace was short and firm, but it felt warm and comfortable. The man put a hand on my shoulder and said "He looks just like you, Dawson."

Dawson sat down on one of the bar stools and ushered me to sit down too. Mr. Chip ordered two more beers, giving a little wink to the young man behind the bar as his cue to ignore the fact that both of us were not old enough to drink in public.

"I remember you and your friends coming here last year, Jesse. Hard to forget a small group of high schoolers stumbling out of the parking lot smelling like the kind of liquor I use to remove stains in my kitchen," Mr. Chip said with a laugh.

I didn't know whether to feel embarrassed or honored that we had made such an impact on the inn's owner. "We were definitely a little messy a year ago, but I assure you there won't be any stumbling around the lobby this time."

My thoughts were interrupted by the smell of what I believed to be a mix of grilled fish, French fries and some sort of soup. I was guessing either cream of mushroom or cream of chicken. The inn had a dining hall in an outdoor patio on the other side of the lawn. It was much smaller the last time I came here with the rest of the guys, so it must have been completely refurbished to look the way it did now. It probably held twice the amount of people and the plastic chairs and dining tables were replaced with beautiful wooden ones. There were fairy lights hanging from the roof, making it look like part of a five-star hotel and not one from a backpacker's inn.

"Why don't you call the rest of them down for dinner? The dining hall has new chefs from the last time you came here, and the menu's pretty damn good," Dawson said, nudging a very proud looking Mr. Chip.

"Dawson came up with the whole idea of sprucing everything up for our dinner menu. Since most of the young ones can't find a bar or club anywhere around this area, he said they might just want to eat somewhere close by so they can get hammered in their rooms as fast as they can," Mr. Chip said, ruffling Dawson's hair playfully. I would have expected Dawson to hate that kind of thing, but all I could see in my brother's face was genuine content. It was almost impossible to not feel the same for him, to think that Dawson came up with a whole idea that was taken into account by the inn amazed me, especially since the idea was panning out so well judging from the amount of people that were following their noses and making their way across the lawn to the food.

"You always had the best ideas, Dawson," I said, giving him a playful punch in the shoulder. "I'm going to call the rest of them down now."

Going up the elevator, I had a million things running through his head. There was faint Balinese music playing all through the lobby. The organic sounds of wood knocking, ringing bells and soothing humming complemented everything that I was feeling. I had a million thoughts running through my head, but it was less confusion and more awe and less fear and more tranquility. I could tell that Dawson was a lot more mature, and going about things on your own like that would obviously make someone look at the world a lot more differently. I had seen his face those months leading up to him leaving and it worried me every single day. Seeing him like this was more than enough for me to believe that whatever he was doing here really was the best for him.

Of course I still strongly disagreed with the way Dawson handled his whole ordeal of running away from home. But I couldn't find a part of myself that disagreed with the reason why Dawson chose to do it. Listening to him explain his decision, looking at him with Mr. Chip, hearing about how he was contributing his ideas for reasons bigger than himself—it made me want those things too, it made me think about what Cassie said about how I looked like I wanted to leave. Maybe that's why Dawson was so eager to keep me out of the loop. The last thing he would have wanted was to have our mother have to deal with both her sons running off in pursuit of answers to their messed up heads.

The elevator door opened and surprisingly, I found myself face-to-face with my friends.

"We were just going to go look for you, it's been hours," Kivo said, his hand awkwardly scratching the back of his neck.

"We're starving too. We ate all the bread," Gryme chimed in.

"Gry ate all of yours," Mo added in a sing-song voice.

"I was just about to call you guys down for dinner. I don't know if you noticed how the dining hall had been reorganized, but it looks great and the food smells amazing," I said with a shy smile, hoping that they got the hint that this was me trying to apologize in the only way I knew how without being too embarrassingly direct.

Cassie walked into the elevator, her hair now freely falling to the small of her back. She was wearing a fitting mustard sundress that seemed a little too feminine for the street style loving girl I was accustomed to. There was really something going on with her.

"We thought you'd never ask," she said with a bright grin.

The walk to the dining hall wasn't a long one, but somehow we managed to cover so much ground about my conversation with Dawson. I was guessing that they must have been walking really slowly.

"I had the inn's number saved from the last time we came here, so you have no idea how confused I was when I got a call from Happy Holiday Inn and picked up to hear Dawson Loo's voice on the other side," Mitchel said.

Mitchel and I had been friends since kindergarten, and it helped keep the friendship going strong since he only lived a few houses away from me. Mitchel was the most mature one in the group, and even though we were all the same age, we always turned to him as though he was five years older and had gone through all our life problems before. Dawson had always trusted Mitchel the most out of all my friends. When Dawson used to be on big brother duty when our mom was out, he would just call Mitchel over to be with me until he came back from a quick night hanging out with his friends. It wasn't surprising to me that Mitchel was the one he reached out to first. From all those times checking in with him throughout the night to make sure that our mom wasn't home yet, I would only expect that Dawson had his number memorized at this point.

"Did you fight with your brother again?" Mitchel had asked me one day last summer. We were walking to the grocery store to get some matches for his father. Unlike most families,

Mitchel's household was against the use of kitchen appliances that might make things easier. I didn't know why or how it started. I never really questioned it until we came over for breakfast one day when we were little kids after some early morning soccer. I remember watching in confusion as he fried their bread on the stovetop to make toast. There were no toasters, fancy stoves, blenders, can openers or anything like that. We were getting matches to light the charcoal-black stove up.

"What?" I replied in confusion, taken aback by such a specific question.

I guess Mitchel had taken notes over the years and realized that any arguments or miscommunication with Dawson always had me feeling a certain type of way. I never looked angry like how most younger brothers might. Instead, my arguments with Dawson made me sad and almost disappointed. "You look like you're a part of a music video about a young boy who thinks he's ugly and useless," Mitchell told me. "I'm not saying that you're ugly and useless, you just look like you think you do. Or you look like Dawson thinks you are."

Mitchell always understood how much I wanted the approval of my brother in a way that not many people did. It was hard for anyone to wrap their head around why I admired Dawson because I never really talked about him to anyone. Maybe

I felt embarrassed about needing an older brother as much as I did. I might have been afraid that Dawson didn't care about our relationship in the same way. Mitchel had come to know about how emotional I could be and how much I craved genuine affection sometimes. He was always listening to me ramble on for hours about people and their connections with each other, all the endless possibilities that exist in the world if somebody just had one person in their life that they would do anything for. Mitchel told me once that he wasn't sure if I was just listening to really sad songs or reading really deep books to keep thinking these things.

"But it's probably because you spend so much time watching how the lack of love and the lies surrounding it had ruined your mom and Dawson in so many ways," he told me. "You're just looking for a way out."

When we walked out of the lobby and made our way to dinner, there was crispness in the air that I never felt anywhere. It suddenly smelled like fresh cut grass and morning dew, which was weird since it was almost 8:30 p.m.. Mitchell gave me firm grab on the shoulder.

"Has Dawson been feeling okay?" he asked me.

"Dawson looks happier don't you think? He always had this kind of scary, grunge, big boy face. But now he kind of looks more like you, Jesse," Kivo said, scrunching his nose up in an attempt to guess what was on the dinner menu that night.

"He does, doesn't he?" I replied. "I had this conversation with him once, and he told me about how lost he was and that he couldn't feel anything about himself. But when I was talking to him just now, I could see in his face the things that he was feeling, the pride and joy. He looked more certain than I've ever seen him."

"Do you think that running away from home was the only way for him to get the chance to feel that way?" Cassie asked. I paused for a moment and shrugged in response. I really had no idea about that.

"Have you ever thought about running away, Jesse?" she continued.

I looked around. I knew how badly everyone wanted an answer by the way they were avoiding my gaze.

"Not like that," I said. That was the best response I could come up with.

CHAPTER 8

IN THE CLOUDS

———

The dinner spread tasted exactly the way it smelled. Compared to the simple fried rice and noodle options that were available for dinner the last time they were here, the options Mr. Chip had come up with alongside Dawson and the rest of the kitchen staff made them feel like they were in a little luxury resort.

Dawson had brought them around the entire dining hall, where long tables on each side of the wall were lined up with trays for guests to grab their food buffet-style. I trailed behind Dawson, gaping the whole time at how he was able to explain each dish and all their ingredients without a hitch or a drop of hesitation.

"I thought you said you were the marketing and design guy, you're telling me you've been cooking too?" I asked in disbelief.

"I can't cook knucklehead. I know my food because I eat well, these muscles aren't going to grow themselves," Dawson took a fat pinch of my arms, completely disregarding my sharp howl of pain. "You need to start eating well too."

We got a table right next to the tray of main entrees, and we found ourselves refilling our plates before we were even done with our food in the first place. It was just too good.

Dawson was working at the lobby for the night, and he said that he would see me in the morning. It was just the six of us in the hotel room after Dawson left, and it had probably just turned 10:00 p.m. Alcohol bottles were lined up on the coffee table, and each one of us were sprawled completely on our beds.

"I can't even look at those bottles right now, I can't imagine any more liquid in my body after all that mushroom soup," Gryme said.

"If Gryme says he can't eat anymore then we know it's a problem," Kivo got off the bed, and reached into his backpack. He pulled out a small clear bag, waving it in the air with a "Yoo-hoo" to get everyone's attention.

It was a small bag of weed, the white transparent plastic filled to the brim with clouds of green. I chewed on my lip nervously, a little worried about getting caught but mostly worried about how it would make me feel. I knew that half the people at this inn were already walking around with heavy-lidded eyes and a slight tremble in their step. I always got anxious whenever I smoked, especially since I've let myself drift into a mindset where I questioned the legitimacy of everything I thought I knew. Sometimes I would be excited about the thought of an escape. I would sit back and let my eyes shut slowly, letting a soft creeping tingle climb up my body like growing vines. I enjoyed the initial minutes, the sweet spot where I allowed myself to forget. I would look around and see everyone doing the same thing. And then I feel myself tumbling. I feel myself falling from the top of a cliff to the ground, a sharp wave of anxiety gripping my shoulders back in my sight to remind me how far away the ground is. It's funny how scared I get considering how my eyes are closed. I can't see any ground, I can't see myself falling. I just know I am. It's dark and I can't open my eyes.

"My boy, Kivo. Always using his rich boy connections for the good of the people," Mitchel said, jumping off the bed and pouncing on the smaller boy for a hug.

I realized that it had been a good amount of time since we last smoked together. It only took a few minutes for our room to be covered with a light fog.

"You're not gonna have any, Jesse?" Cassie asked. She was sitting across from me, her eyebrows a little furrowed. She must have realized how I was shifting uncomfortably in my seat, contemplating seriously about taking a puff or not. "You don't have to if you don't want to, I promise it's no big deal" she continued, resting her chin in her palms and giving me a warm child-like smile. I knew it was starting to hit her if she was acting like this, a little sweet and more so cute. I blinked a couple times, trying to keep my eyes from lingering on her face. This was a weird feeling to have.

Maybe it was those few seconds of letting me look at one of my best friends that way, actually realizing that she was probably one of the most beautiful girls I had ever come across in town. I was always suffocated by routine, held down by the weight of knowing what was going to happen next and what I was going to feel about it, but I wasn't in any sort of routine right now. I was living in a moment that was new and unexpected. I didn't want to let it go to waste because I was scared. I also really wanted to get that thought of Cassie out of my mind.

"Pass it to me," I said, reaching my hand out to get the blunt from Mitchel. I took a deep inhale, feeling the smoke climb up my nostrils and slowly crawl down my throat. I erupted into a fit of coughs, thumping my hand repeatedly on my chest as the rest of them laughed at me. I rolled my eyes and passed the blunt on, with a smile on my face.

The room had one window that we opened slightly to let the fresh air in, but there was no wind coming through our floor at this point in the night. We had no choice but to brace the smell of old musty wood and sheets blended in with the strong stench being spread across the room by the smoke.

"We have illegal particles basking on every inch of our body, guys," Gryme said. "We're going to be stuck in this room all night waiting for it to wear off."

I actually had no problem with that. My eyelids were getting a little heavier with each blink, and I was stuck thinking about whether the smooth cold texture beneath my feet was ceramic tiles or just my own skin. I seemed to have finally noticed the walls of the room we were staying in, slowly standing up and straight and turning in a slow circle as I looked at every corner of the room carefully. Each white wall was decorated with murals, big and small. I remember it being one of the inn's best charms, rooms decorated by their own backpacker guests. That was what caught our interest about it the first time we came across this place online.

The wall with the window was simply covered in messages and doodles by previous guests that had been here. There were the typical "Jessica loves Anthony" drawings, the "Sarah was here" one-liners, drawings of stick figures under the sun and plates of local food that were definitely drawn by foreigners. I hadn't even realized that I walked off to stare blankly at the wall, my fingertips brushing against each stain of ink on the white cement.

"It's pretty cool isn't it?" Cassie asked, standing next to me. "It's kinda scary too. Who knows the kind of people they were, what their day was going like the day they wrote these, what was on their minds, what they wanted to do next once they checked out."

Cassie had a point. It was just a wall, but it was giving complete strangers a window to communicate with each other. It was allowing strangers to make assumptions about their lives. What if Jessica loved Anthony only to find out that Anthony was going to break up with her a few months later? What if Sarah was here but mentally, she was clocked out somewhere else, worrying about getting a job and paying off student loans? All the stories on this wall were keyholes looking into bigger things, bigger lives.

"We should do one," I said abruptly.

"Do what?" Cassie asked. She was no stranger to my random thoughts, let alone when I was high. I could always trust her to listen to my craziest ideas or dreams without a single word of judgement, when she was in a good mood of course. She looked genuinely confused at what I meant, but there was a sparkle in her eye that seemed like it was pushing me to keep going, almost asking me to keep going with what I was saying.

"You have this look in your eye that I miss," she continued. "Remember how I met you? You were laughing so loud during assembly when I was lined up next to you. You were with the rest of the boys and you turned to me and noticed how pissed I looked, and you said sorry with the cheesiest grin on your face."

The rest of them laughed, shouting out their agreement at how loud I always was during the worst times and at the worst places. Assembly always dragged on so long with announcements from teachers and other students who had dumb things to say about their clubs and sport meets. I was always so restless. I chuckled lightly just thinking about how many times I got into trouble for talking too much or for making weird noises when I tried to hold my laughter.

"We should paint our own mural on one of the walls here!" I shouted and my hands stretched out animatedly. I mimicked a paint brush sweeping across the walls and everyone burst into laughter. Something about hearing it that made me want to make my movements even bigger, stretch my arms out even wider or jump around the room if I could.

"I have the artistic capability of a fish, but I'll let that be my creative authenticity. What's the plan, Jesse boy?" Gryme said, motioning for everyone to huddle together in the middle of the room. Our heads and arms were messily brushing against each other, some of us struggling to keep our balance.

In a room that seemed like it was spinning, I never had a clearer idea of what I wanted to see when we painted that wall. I wanted six little squares lined up in a row on the wall, each for us to fill up.

"That sounds great, Jesse. But why don't we do things a little different," Mo said. "Why don't we have one big box for you that you'll finish first, a box for you to fill up with everything you want and think about and are scared of, you've always been the better one at expressing yourself, and I want you to have the biggest chance to. I'm sure we can all agree."

The rest of them nodded, pulling me closer into the huddle and giving me playful little slaps on the back.

"Then when you're done, we'll all fill up the spaces we have around it," Mo continued.

"Really, I don't know, I want it to be something for all of us," I said slowly, a smile tugging at the edge of my lips at the thought of them talking about how much I did actually enjoy expressing myself. I used to make them all listen to me talk about movie scenes, song lyrics and artwork. I would have all these huge ideas about writing music and filming videos that would focus on the deeper meaning of things. I wanted something raw and unscripted, something that could never be staged or retaken again. How a picture remains a printed picture when it falls out of a polaroid camera, and how people can't delete it and pretend it never happened. I wanted to see the mistakes, the candid joy and the things that people thought they didn't see just because they were too busy thinking about the things they wanted to see. I loved looking into how people used language and visuals to implicitly express the highs and lows they were feeling. With all the noise and the talking around me, I sat down on the bed just to pause for a moment.

I used to paint and I used to try writing songs, telling myself that they were great even though they probably sounded like the writing of a ten-year-old kid. I used to do a lot more things than just lay in my bed and stare at my ceiling wondering why things felt so wrong.

"Doing this for yourself is the biggest thing you could do for us right now," Mitchel said.

They were serious about this. They were serious about me. How distant had I really been this whole time? Did they really feel like they had lost me?

"I'll do it for you guys then," I said.

Then there was a loud knock on the door that made us jump, our panicked eyes shifting nervously to look at the smoke that was still floating around the room. I tried rubbing my eyes, hoping that the blurriness I was seeing was just from the fact that my eyes felt really dry.

"It's not your eyes man, there's a whole lot of smoke in here," Kivo whispered, making his way to the door like he was on a stealth mission. He held onto the doorknob tightly, peering carefully through the eyehole in the door. "W-Who is it?" he asked, using all his strength to not sound like he was floating through a different dimension.

Behind him, the rest of the boys were doubling over at the crack in Kivo's voice. Cassie stood unfazed, holding her breath to make sure that nobody punched their way through the door and hurt Kivo. If the guys weren't going to protect their little trooper, she definitely was. She protected everyone. And as much as Kivo says he hated how she mothered him so much, he would be lying if he said he didn't want her to. Being around boys all the time gets pretty annoying.

"It's just me. You sound high as hell, Kivo. Open up."

Kivo cleared his throat, opening the door to see Dawson standing there with bags of chips and bars of chocolate. "I would be worried if you guys didn't end up needing these," Dawson looked around the smoky room, and the rest of them standing still at the very center. Seeing my brother in the doorway, I gave him a toothy grin and a little wave of my fingers.

"You smoked enough for an army in here," he said, laughing.

Dawson placed the snacks on the table, right by the untouched bottles of alcohol. I forgot we even had those.

"Hey, we have something to ask you," I said.

"What is it?"

"Can you ask Mr. Chip if we can paint something on one of the walls in the inn?"

Dawson smiled. "There's an empty half of the wall right there," he said, pointing to the far end of the room at an empty white patch next to Mo's bed. "I'll ask Mr. Chip in the morning and let you guys know. He's always excited about having people paint new stuff. I'm kind of surprised you want to do that."

Dawson held onto my arm for a quick squeeze. For some reason, I started to feel a little emotional, a swell forming in my throat. I almost forgot how great it felt to have a brother around.

"Now that Dawson doesn't look scary anymore, you both really do look alike," Gryme said inaudibly as he chewed on a handful of chips in his mouth. "Do you wanna smoke with us?"

"And you're still the same old Gry," Dawson said, shaking his head as he made his way out the door. "I have an early shift tomorrow so I'll let you guys have fun on your own tonight."

*　*　*

Jesse was the first person to fall asleep as expected. He had smoked more and ended up not even being able to stand up while the others danced and sang to their indie rock playlist. There was something about those songs that made everything pop a little more—the colors in the room, the smells and the sounds. There was something about the way "Last Nite" by The Strokes sounded when it blasted through a room with just the six of them. The heavy guitar riffs drowned out everything besides the world that they were living in at that moment, and sometimes that selective perception was necessary to keep things in check, to keep their heads and their hearts secure. The six of them had always lived in their own little world because they wanted to see reality from a different window that was a little more daring, a little more unrealistic and a lot slower. In their own little world time was relative, things didn't move as fast, they didn't have to keep up with expectations and they didn't need to come back to their problems. They were just present in a really long paused moment where nothing else moved but them.

"I think we should just let Jesse draw the mural on his own," Mo said. He was sitting on one of the plastic chairs that he had brought up to the room with his legs perched up on the edge of Kivo's bed.

He had seen Jesse paint on his own once by accident, and he was pretty sure he was the only one that had ever seen him doing anything like that. Mo always liked to show up at Jesse's uninvited on the most random days. His mother would hear the bell ring four times in unison and yell out "Mo's here!" up the stairs without even needing to look outside. Jesse had his earphones on so loud one day that he couldn't hear any of his mom's calls. She had let Mo in, warning him that Jesse wasn't answering and that she didn't know if he was busy upstairs. Mo tried to stifle a smile as he nodded and walked up the stairs, trying to plan a way to burst into the room and catch Jesse with his hands in his pants without actually having to see anything.

"HAH!" Mo yelled as he flung the bedroom door open with his hands over his eyes.

"You have got to be kidding me, I told you to text me next time!" Jesse yelled back, picking up an upside down paper plate that had fallen to the ground and smeared blotches of paint all over his wooden floors. Mo had his head tilted to the side, his eyebrows furrowed as he stared at a brown square stuck with duct tape on one of Jesse's bedroom walls.

"What's that?" Mo asked, walking toward it. It was one side of a large cardboard box that had been ripped out. "You paint?" He let his eyes trace the soft black outlines that travelled across the smooth brown surface. The black outlines met to make the shape of something that looked like a long dress. It looked both realistic yet abstract, with the spaces between the outlines still half-filled with a burst of different purple and yellow. The two colors seemed like they would never go together, but somehow they both met at the waist of the dress in a soft blurry cloud of contrasts. There was no head, just arms and legs coming out of the fabric, positioned in a way that made the incomplete figure look like it was running. Its arms and legs bent so awkwardly that Mo couldn't help but stare.

"You're not supposed to see this, it's terrible. Jesus, you're relentless, why can't you just text me?"

Mo watched as Jesse flailed around the room in a panic, stashing his paint brushes in random drawers and storming over to the wall to rip the painting off.

"You need to relax, Jesse," Mo said, scurrying over to stand in front of the wall and in Jesse's way. "I don't know why you're acting like you just murdered someone, but whatever this weird thing is that you just painted, it looks like some legit artist shit. Like those things you see in really cool exhibits but nobody really knows what their about."

Jesse sighed, his eyes darting around the room because Mo was staring right at him and he didn't really want to do the same. "I just grabbed shit from the bookstore the other day because I felt like painting for some reason, it was so weird." Jesse walked toward his bed and sat down, pointing at the paint brushes, sketching paper, paint tubes and drawing tutorial books laying out all across the room.

"I was at the store and there was this really tall lady in this weird purple and yellow dress, and she was straight up running out the doors because apparently she left her wallet at the restaurant next door. It was just kind of funny even though it wasn't. I don't want to sound like this stupid kid but it was just her facial expression, the weird outfit, the way that she was so awkwardly tall it made her limbs kind of fall weirdly around her. The image just stuck in my head," Jesse said.

Mo remembered that afternoon so well. He had spent the next couple hours blasting music in Jesse's room as he continued painting. It had always felt like such a defining moment in their friendship, especially because Mo had always felt like he wasn't as pulled into the group as everyone else. He didn't like playing soccer with them or even hanging out together every night. He was always a little more reserved and unlike the others, he enjoyed time alone more than they did. That afternoon with Jesse felt so easy, it felt even better that he learned something new about a friend that he had known for years. It helped him remember how easy their friendship as a group was even though they liked different things and had expressed themselves differently. Jesse had made him promise not to tell anyone else about the painting because he was shy and he didn't want anybody trying to make him paint stuff for fun.

When Jesse had suggested the mural, Mo couldn't stop a smile from spreading across his face. He knew how happy it made Jesse feel and he could tell that Jesse had probably not touched his little stash of paint brushes in a while.

"I think we should just leave the room and let Jesse use up as much of the wall as he needs. I'm sure he's going to realize that he needs a lot more space than just one big square," Mo said, turning to the rest of them who were all lying down on Gryme's bed. Jesse's snores were echoing in the room at that point.

"Speaking of leaving the room, where are Cass and Mitch?" Gryme asked, jumping up from his position on the bed.

"It was the three of us and Jesse this whole time?" Kivo asked, staggering as he tried to lift his head off the pillow. His eyes were so red and puffy they took up almost half of his small face. "We really are the dumbest ones in the group."

"I don't know how to take this kind of information," Mo said slowly.

"Let's just...go to sleep. I don't want to think about this, it's weird" Gryme said, lowering his head on his pillow as Kivo dragged his feet to the other side of the room and fell face first on his own bed.

CHAPTER 9

THE BOX

———

"Put your brain in a box. Stack the images you have in your mind up, face down, like they're in picture frames you want to set aside just for a little while," a voice said.

I was in a dark room with a single light focused in the very middle. The walls of the room were a clear white, but the uneven lighting made it look grey. In the center of the room was a white plastic chair with a pale red box on it. It had white ribbons undone by its side.

I walked closer to the box. It was funny how the closer I got to it, the smaller it became.

"Put those images in there," the voice said again. "You need to put away the things you don't need. You're moving away, and you need to make space for new pictures. Forget the ones you want to forget."

"The box is too small. I can't fit the pictures in there," I said in a whisper. I looked into what was now a cube no bigger than the size of my palm. It was dark inside, and I could hear my whisper echoing back at me. If I dropped something in there, it was probably never going to come back.

"The things you want to forget will always fit in there. You just need to shrink them, fold them up, or tear them into pieces. You're storing unnecessary things as a whole, and they're too big. They're eating up too much space."

The voice was starting to sound familiar.

* * *

I woke up panting, bringing the back of my hand up to wipe a small amount of sweat beading at my forehead. I always had the same dream most nights, a dark room, a box and a voice.

I was always asked to store pictures away. It was an interesting analogy that I now seemed to understand as I stared at a different ceiling, one that wasn't the same pale yellow that I was used to from my room. The pictures were fragments of my mind, distorted versions of reality that were stained by my negative perceptions and hatred of my own emotions. The voice was asking me to let go of these tainted images. It was asking me to empty them into this box that I now know would never run out of space, because it was so deep it almost looked like it was leading me to a tunnel that never ended.

I usually never made it to the center of the room. I would always wake up panting before I was even remotely halfway to reaching the box that I could store my thoughts in and keep them out of my way. This was the closest that I had ever gotten to it, but it shrank. Or maybe these images were too big because I refused to fold them and throw them away. I let them take up too much space in my mind.

But it felt like I was getting closer to dropping them down that tunnel.

I still felt like I was floating, my fingers and toes tingling. It was also the best sleep I had in months, the first night where I didn't have to force myself to clear my head and not succumb to racing thoughts. Weird dream aside, I felt pretty well rested.

There was a fresh breeze that kept sweeping through the window, so the room was somewhat cold. I sat up, bringing the thin cotton blanket up to my chest and wrapping myself in it. Everyone else was still sleeping, and besides Cassie, they were all snoring obnoxiously loud. Choosing the bed next to Gryme was like choosing to sleep next to a running tractor. I counted myself lucky that the weed had gotten to me so hard that I couldn't even hear a thing. I heard everything a little too clearly now.

I slowly got off the bed, tip-toeing my way to the door and opening it slowly so the sunlight from outside wouldn't pierce into the room. There was a dark blue curtain over the window that surprisingly kept the room dark even though it let all the wind in. I looked down at my arms and legs and noticed that I was wearing an old Iron Man shirt that I got as a gift from my grandma, paired with a pair of faded torn-up basketball shorts. I didn't remember how I even managed to change into my sleeping attire, but it was so comfortable that I really didn't care how embarrassing it might possibly look for a teenage boy to walk around the lobby looking like this.

"You're up so early. You also look like a seven-year-old," Dawson said, walking up to me. He had a basket of pastries in his hand and pointed to a croissant that sat right at the top of the pile. "It's filled with chocolate and it has a really flakey pastry. If my memory serves me right, that's your favorite kind."

"Good morning to you too," I answered with a yawn, realizing that he wasn't all too sure what time it was. "And what time is it now anyway?"

"It's 7:30 a.m."

I nodded as I took the croissant, barely waiting a few seconds before taking a big bite out of it. I didn't remember how much of the chips and chocolate I had last night. All I knew was that there was a mountain of empty packets in the trash this morning, but I still felt like there was a gaping hole in my stomach begging to be filled. I had never been happier to hear Dawson say that there was a breakfast spread in the dining hall with lots more croissants where that came from.

"Are you just going door to door delivering pastries? Because that's one thing I never expected to see from you in my life," I chuckled as my brother rolled his eyes. He handed me the rest of the pastries.

"One of the guests on this floor ordered an extra bucket, but his kind soul decided to give it to me instead of exchanging it for something else. You guys can have it though," Dawson said.

"They're definitely going to need it."

"I asked Mr. Chip about painting the room and he's cool with it. I have a bunch of art stuff lying around in the storage room that you can use," Dawson said, a big smile spreading across his face.

I widened my eyes, swallowing a whole chunk of croissant without even chewing. I had almost forgotten about my idea to paint on the inn's wall. I recalled staring at the messages and doodles around the window, completely mesmerized by the way that all these different words and drawings came together to create a big, cohesive picture. Last night, under the influence of false confidence not projected by my sober mind, I suppose I thought that I could create something just as moving. Something that would make a person pause and look if they walked past it, enveloped by curiosity as they tried to understand the meaning behind the things thrown around in front of them.

I wasn't so sure about that idea anymore. The magic about those doodles on the wall were that they were kind of like Polaroid pictures—they were unscripted, sprawled in ink over cement in instant thought translating into messy words, stick figures and symbols that weren't planned or painted with precision. I remember wanting to recreate that. But would sitting down in front of a wall with paint supplies give me that or will it just make me think so much about the idea of making it so perfect that I end up with nothing?

"You don't look too excited, you were practically jumping when you asked me yesterday," Dawson said with a concerned look on his face.

"It's just…the idea of doing it seemed so much more possible last night with all the smoke in my face," I paused, looking out over the edge at a group of young girls who were running onto the lawn with matching bikini tops under denim overalls. They had paint on their faces and on their fingertips, speaking quickly in a language I couldn't understand as they laughed.

Dawson turned his head to look at the same direction. "Trust me, those girls have no artistic sense whatsoever, the puppy they drew looks like a chicken," he said. "I know you have a wild imagination. We don't need something that's going to go up in a museum and we don't need you to spend hours on it. Just grab a brush and some paint and do whatever your head tells you to do; movie scenes, song lyrics or your kind of thing."

"My kind of thing," I repeated softly, my eyes still fixed on the lawn. I let my gaze rest on the deck chair that I had sat out on to watch the sunset after I initially saw Dawson the day before.

They're eating up too much space. That one line from my dream had stuck with me. I needed to clear some space and talk to Dawson about what was going on.

"Dawson, can I talk to you for a little bit? I just need to ask you a few things that I've been meaning to ask," I told him.

He looked completely taken off guard, but he nodded almost immediately. He motioned for me to follow him down the stairs. He was heading to the lobby for his next shift at the reception counter, but he apparently finished delivering pastries early and had some time to spare.

When we got down to the lobby, Tony was sitting behind the counter too. He looked over at us like an excited puppy, waving his arms in the air. I noticed how Dawson beamed at the sight of him, waving back with just as much vigor.

We headed outside, walking out to the far left of the lawn where the building structure ended. The side of the inn was decorated with potted bougainvilleas on a path of white and black stones. Dawson sat on the cement floor by the stones, wrapping his arms around his knees. I sat next to him and did the same.

"What is it that you wanted to ask me?"

I took a deep breath, collecting my questions into a compact little mental pouch. I wanted to keep it straight to the point. I didn't want to overwhelm him, and I guess I didn't want to overwhelm myself too. I had to fold things up, make them small enough to clear my head while fitting them into a shrinking box.

"I guess there are three main things. How were you really after you left, considering how I knew you weren't acting like yourself the months leading up to it? How did you meet Tony? And does mom know where you are?"

I expected Dawson to falter just a little, perhaps even try to avoid my question. Much to my surprise, he shifted his body around to face me firmly.

"I'll sum it up to you in one story. I hope this answers your questions, because honestly, there's nothing much left that I can say about it anymore. I think you know what I mean when I say that the same story I repeat, the same feelings I repeat start to get old. I wanted to move on, and this is my only way of doing so," he said.

I nodded. The voice in my dream was starting to sound a lot like Dawson.

"When I left the house, I didn't have much clue on where to go. I took my friend's car up to the bus stop near his house, and I hopped on the first bus I saw. I told you about the tourists I met who introduced me to this place, but I actually met Tony first. He was at the bus stop, he had a bunch of bags strapped on him and he looked just as lost as I was. Only I looked a lot more of a mess than he did."

Dawson picked up a rock and let it rest on his palm, his fingers gripping the smooth surface.

"I hadn't been myself because I really didn't feel like I was. I had lots of voices in my head telling me that I wasn't good enough. I was crying a lot, throwing my pillow against the wall in the middle of the night to let out my frustration. I was just sad and angry because I felt like I was going nowhere, and everything at home needed saving but I didn't know if I could do it if I was feeling this way. I needed help that I refused to get. I needed to talk to someone but I refused to, I felt like my problems weren't really problems," he continued.

I understood him. I really did.

"When Tony found me at the bus stop, I had dark circles under my eyes from no sleep and lots of angry tears. He doesn't have a family, he's gone through quite some shit and he's been working at different motels and inns to make a living after he left his foster house. He saw me and I guess he knew what I was feeling. My problems were nothing compared to his, but he told me when somebody needs to fix themselves it didn't matter how big or serious the problem was. Things like that aren't relative, their specific to you. They hurt for you and it doesn't matter how small it might seem to other people, it takes a toll on people differently."

Nothing amazed me more than how calm he sounded telling me all of this. Like the voice in my dream, it was as though he really had managed to fold the images that he didn't need and get rid of them. He was able to move on to better things. It took him a long time. It took leaving everything that he was comfortable with behind, but sometimes that was the only way to get rid of the things a person is uncomfortable with. He was learning that he was capable of so much more than he knew.

"Mom knows where I am," he said slowly. "I didn't want you to know and I'm sorry about that. I didn't even want her to know."

I could see his eyes getting wet. I could see that he never stopped thinking about her. He just didn't want to give her more reasons to hurt and blame herself for not giving him enough. As painful as this may have been for her, I knew that it was the only way that he could find his own way back to her as the son he always wanted to be.

"She wanted me to get help, talk to someone professionally but I didn't want to and I text her every week to let her know that I'm sleeping well, eating well and that I think about her every day."

He smiled at me, resting his arm on my knees and nudging me playfully.

"I'm still the man of the house. I'm just trying to be better."

* * *

There were brushes, paint buckets and strips of old white cloth laid out all over the floor. They had all pushed aside all the beds by that empty spot in the wall. I stood in front of it, taking in what was now going to be my empty canvas.

"Do you know what you're going to do with it?" Cassie asked.

"Sort of…" I replied, picking up the thickest brush I could find.

"Alright, I think we should all leave you to it and come back in an hour to see the progress," Mitchell stood up, with Cassie following right after as she grabbed her purse off the coffee table.

The rest of the boys looked at the two of them in confusion. "Were we supposed to go somewhere?"

"We have a free hour you guys can go wherever you want," Cassie said nonchalantly, making her way to the door.

"A free hour, we don't have any plans in general, we've been free," Kivo said, stepping closer to Cassie and Mitchell. The two of them backed away, not looking at each other even once. I sat still, lips pursed and eyes slowly widening as I realized what was going on. I remembered looking at Cassie the night before and thinking to myself that I was stupid for not realizing how beautiful she really was. The pieces of the puzzle were starting to fall into place. It wasn't that I had been ignoring her the whole time, I just always found her beautifully amazing. She was just going the extra mile this trip—dressing up, straightening and curling her hair and walking around with a little skip in her step. She wasn't doing this to impress someone she was heightening a sense of confidence that was already there. She was reminding someone that she was in the room, happy and glowing.

The radiance bouncing off her was so bright that it felt like it was aimed at me just because I was in her line of sight. That someone was actually Mitchell. I could tell from the way he refused to take his eyes off the ground, since Cassie was standing right in front of him in a baby blue dress that was definitely new.

"So where are you and Mitchell going?" Gryme asked, raising an eyebrow.

Mitchell was standing awkwardly with his hands by his sides. Cassie was taking a little too long to put on her shoes without laces. Gryme, Kivo and Mo were standing frozen in place, the three musketeers of making every situation as uncomfortable as it could possibly be. I wondered how far the four of us could push it until we actually managed to catch them in a position they didn't want to be caught in.

"I'm going to the lawn to read my book," Cassie said.

"And I'm going to catch up with Dawson downstairs, maybe get some advice about breaking into the business world with all the contacts he now has or all the people he's met and stuff," Mitchel said. The end of his sentence trailed off into a quiet buzz that weighed the air in the room down with an almost nervous sense of silence.

"Breaking into the business world," I whispered in disbelief. I caught Mitchel in the corner of my eye cursing under his breath. Even he knew how dumb he must have sounded.

"Alright then you guys go ahead. Read your book and get business advice like any normal teen would on a trip with their friends," Mo said his voice so monotonous that I had to bite a knuckle to keep from smirking. "Me, Kivo and Gryme are going to get drunk, so that by the time we come back to the room we're ready to be sucked into the portal, that is, Jesse Loo's creative capabilities."

All five of them made their way to the door.

"When we come back, you're getting drunk too," Kivo called out as he left the room.

I threw two thumbs up in the air as a response, and then turned around to face my blank canvas again. I suddenly knew exactly where to start.

CHAPTER 10

FINDING ANSWERS

—

I would think that I was always a romantic at heart. I liked love songs, the ones that made it sound like I was on board a train in the middle of a field of pink lilies. I also liked the ones about heartbreak, maybe even a little more than I liked the ones about falling in love. I had a profound interest in the way people acted when they were in love, the way their hands brushed against each other, the way their eyes melted together in a common gaze or the way their voices lowered into a whisper when they're alone. What interested me more was the way people acted when they were falling in love with someone they felt they couldn't have.

I had never been in too many relationships. The last girl I dated was when I was 14, and it was a chaotic mess of infatuation, short-lived passion and a deluded under-standing of what a relationship was supposed to mean. She made me feel a rush of adrenaline. We would sneak out of school every Friday during recess to go to a park nearby. There was an old gazebo by the swings that always smelled like grass after the rain, and I would take her hand and run in there with music blasting from my beat up phone speakers. She liked to sing, and she was great at it. I would lean against the wall of the gazebo, watching as she twirled around in her school uniform, her fist balled into an imaginary microphone as her soft voice tangled itself in the air around me.

I remembered asking myself, "Is this what love feels like?" But with every dumb fourteen-year-old fight about not replying to texts soon enough and helping other girls with homework, it was clear that being in love didn't mean that I wanted my entire relationship to be a moment in a gazebo.

I wanted the blank wall in front of me to be a lot of things, but I honestly believed that art always flowed better when it started with the functional dysfunctionalities of love in all its painful beauty.

I dipped a thick brush into a bucket of black paint, and pressed a big blotch into the wall, keeping the brush fixed in its place.

"When I draw this line, there's no going back. I'm gonna have to keep going," I muttered under my breath.

Little drops of black paint were starting to drip off the tip of the brush into a little pool on the old newspapers laid out on the ground. I slowly pulled my brush upwards, leaving a thick black line behind it all the way from the bottom of the wall to the very middle of it.

No going back now. For the first time in a long time, I felt like I had to be completely honest. With paint on the wall and no cream colored paint to attempt hiding anything I could potentially ruin, there was no way for me to just walk away and leave a half-completed painting on the wall of a tourist hotel. I was going to let myself remember every memory, even the ones I didn't want.

Carefully, I let my brush outline the frame of a patio. The girl didn't play a significant role in my life whatsoever, but I had to give her credit for teaching me to get in tune with myself. She helped me realize that I had feelings, and in fact, I had a lot of them.

I wasn't sure how much time had passed. It felt like hours before I heard a small "Can I come in?" whisper from the far end of the room. I was half expecting it to be my friends banging on the door impatiently to see what I had been up to, but I also had the feeling that they were going to give me much more time than just an hour.

Dawson peeked his head through the door giving me a toothy little grin, Mitchel's business talk must have bored him.

I paused for a second, unsure if having him there would help me open up my creativity, or if the added pressure would just limit the mural to black lines that somewhat looked like a house with no walls.

"Fine, fine," I finally said, laughing as Dawson took offense to the minutes of hesitation.

"Is that the outdoor patio thing in the park near our house?" Dawson stood in front of the wall, the same toothy grin from earlier still on his face.

I stopped and took a couple steps backward to where he was standing in the room. I didn't realize that I had been painting for so long that it covered almost half the entire wall. I hadn't taken a pause this entire time to stop and look at everything I was doing. From where I was standing right in front of the wall, the painting was stretched out wide, almost as wide as it would be if I was standing with both my arms straightened out to the sides.

The structure was relatively easy to recognize despite how I thought that it looked like a messy intersection of lines. In fact, I was completely taken aback that Dawson could recognize it so easily.

"Oh wow…" I said. "You know what it is."

"I told you, Jesse. You're good."

The messy intersection of lines actually did look very much like the structure that constantly appeared in my daydreams. I had painted the back of a young boy's head standing right in the middle of it, looking out into what looked like a field of flowers. All the flowers were drawn differently, and they were all different kinds. I drew roses, lilies, sunflowers and daisies. Splashes of color filled the right side of the wall where the flowers were, the sky above the field and one side of the patio painted to fit the color of a dripping sunset. Light pink and orange hues that gradually faded and blended in with the pale green of the grass.

"How did you get that ugly old green to look like that?" Dawson asked.

I shrugged. "I mixed it with a bunch of yellow and white, I surprised myself there too."

Dawson nodded, his eyes fixed on the figures standing at the very corner of the field. They were grey silhouettes with minute feature distinctions that made it easy for him to recognize exactly who it was. The taller one was Dawson and I assumed he could tell from the excessively broad shoulders.

The shorter figure next to that was a woman, whose head was tilted upwards to look at him. There was a small ponytail perched high on her head, and she was wearing a skirt that flowed to right below her knees. That was our mother.

"Why the field?" Dawson asked, stepping closer to the mural.

I watched as he crouched down to take a closer look at the flowers. Daisies were our mother's favorite. She would wake up every Saturday morning, make a cup of coffee and head out to the market to get a fresh bunch alongside the rest of the groceries. She would put them in a vase by a framed wedding picture of her with our father, which sat on a coffee table next to our large living room window. I did say that Saturdays were the worst. I would come downstairs to the afternoon sunlight cast brightly over the daisies and the photograph. My mom would be seated right across from it with a magazine or newspaper in her hand. I knew she was just using it as a decoy. She would never read any of it, but just gaze longingly at the table under the sunlight.

"Sometimes I wished it wasn't just daisies that she brought home every Saturday," I said slowly, as though my words were making circles around a very fragile, thin piece of ice. "I wanted different flowers and different colors. Our whole house was stuck on the same memory. I felt like she was stuck in a time loop that replayed every time she brought home another bunch of the same white daisies."

Dawson turned around to face me, before slowly sitting down on the ground with his elbows perched on both his knees. "You don't really remember much about dad do you?"

"I don't really care. I don't think he was worth remembering much, don't you think?" I said. I sat down on the ground too, eyes fixed on my paint-stained fingers. "I painted her looking up at you because the last thing she needed was for you to leave home. I understand why it was necessary, and I know she knew too. But we both know how she takes things like this."

I watched Dawson's shoulders start to tense. He knew that I loved him, but he also had to know that expressing the anger I felt toward him like this was my way of throwing unwanted images down an endless tunnel.

"The field...is the new memories I want her to make, memories I want us to make as a family. We don't need to burn the daisies to move on we just need more flowers, flowers to symbolize joy instead of loss. And she needs you to do that. She needs you to come home, if not for good, then just for a little while until she can understand what it's like to let you go the right way."

I had a lot of doubts about saying the things I just said. I would never want to hurt my brother, but I knew that he was waiting for the right kind of push to bring him back. He said it himself that he thought about her every day, and I could tell that he was almost ready as a man, but not ready enough to face the woman that he cared about most. The time loop that our little family was stuck in affected each of us in different ways. It made our mother numb, it made me feel more than I should feel and it made Dawson start looking for a place in the world, somewhere far from the loop, no matter what the cost.

Dawson slowly inched forward to sit next to me, putting a large hand on the back of my head and gently using his fingers to stroke my hair.

I was slightly taken aback at the hand on the back of my head. It was a gesture that was comforting but unfamiliar, and that made me weary even though I didn't want to be. It almost felt too good to be true. Dawson had hit me on the head a million times already throughout our lives, but he had never done this. There was something about it that calmed me down, something that made me want to open the gates that I felt were so tightly bound against me. I leaned my head onto Dawson's shoulder and all of a sudden I felt like a little boy again. A little boy that ran to his older brother whenever his soccer ball flew out of the field, or when he scraped a knee.

Dawson said that our dad used to do the same thing to him before I was born. Whenever he stubbed a toe, or didn't get what he wanted, the poker faced man would sit on the couch and usher for Dawson to come sit in his lap. He would put his hand on the back of his son's head and stroke it slowly.

It was the only form of affection that our dad ever showed him, and he only remembered getting it when he was very little. I didn't remember me getting the same treatment at all, but I suppose I came into his life at the wrong time. He wasn't ready to give out more warm embraces anymore. He was long gone. I don't remember getting any sort of affection or any loving embrace when our dad walked out the door with all of his stuff loaded up in the back of our family's only car.

"I'll do something about it. I won't abandon this family, but I can't abandon myself either. I'll fix this, I promise."

I believed him. He was the only person I could ever put so much trust in.

CHAPTER 11

HOPE

———

I forgot how loud my friends were until I heard them come up the stairs and wait outside the room door. I suddenly felt a little bad for everyone we had ever sat next to in a restaurant or train.

"How long are you going to take finishing this up? I don't want to rush you, but someone's going to file a noise complaint if they're out in the corridor any longer," Dawson said. I was standing by the door, my arm on my hip just waiting to push the door open and startle them to silence. "I'm just doing my job, Jesse," he said with a feigned grin.

"I just need to finish this part it'll only take a minute," I said, my hands working fast on a small empty patch of concrete wall. I dipped a thick brush into a mixture of blue and white paint, swiftly working my brush into little circles on a piece of cardboard that I had been using as my palette.

The voices were muffled outside the room, but it was still loud enough for me to hear everything they were saying rather clearly.

"I don't think I've ever been more excited in my life," Gryme said, pacing up and down with his eyes locked on their room door the whole time. "I better be a big part of this mural thing. I would love if my face was just like front and center but I don't think Jesse draws that well."

"Your face is way too complex for any artist," Kivo said. He sounded like he was stuffing half a croissant from his front jeans pocket into his mouth. He probably had a stash of croissants in his backpack. He loved breakfast buffets.

"Have you guys seen Cassie and Mitch?" Mo asked.

"There's clearly something going on between them, do they think we're dumb?" Gryme said.

"Maybe a little…" Kivo replied.

"Has he opened the door yet?" Cassie's voice boomed out of nowhere. "I stole us some croissants!"

Kivo gasped and opened his backpack for her to see. "I did too!"

I finally cracked my head through the gap. "You guys are too loud, I can't bring you anywhere."

The rest of them screamed my name in unison, before quickly shushing each other up.

"Is it ready?" Mitchell asked, standing right in front of the door almost as though he was going to barge right in regardless of anything I told him.

I slowly opened the door with a sheepish smile on my face, bringing a hand to nervously scratch the back of my neck. "It's done."

They made their way into the room with slow and careful footsteps, all the hyper activeness drained out of sight. They were holding their breath, excited but afraid. This didn't feel like watching a best friend display an art piece at an exhibition. This mural was bigger than all of us, it was bigger than just art—it was them trying to give me, their best friend, some space to breathe. It was them trying to show me that I was more than just a boy from a complicated family in a small town with big dreams that seemed impossible to achieve.

As they walked into the room, the first thing that caught their eye was the splashes of color in the very corner, from the field of flowers.

They slowly made their way to the center of the floor, standing right in front of the colors that spread across half the entire wall. I watched as my friends stared in silence, some of them pursing their lips together into a small smile. I didn't know if I was giving myself too much credit, but they looked like they were going to cry.

"I never knew you could draw like this," Mo said, staring blankly at the wall in front of him before looking at everyone like he was desperately hoping that they didn't know about this too.

"Honestly, neither did I," I said with a slight laugh. I really was genuinely surprised. From thinking about it when I was smoking weed, to actually going through with it, coming up with an idea for it and then finally painting half a whole wall in a span of six hours—nothing about this was normal for me. In fact, I didn't think anything about this was really normal at all.

These past few days were the most spontaneous days I've had in such a long time. I wasn't doing things that I already knew what to expect from. I wasn't looking for questions that I already knew the answers to. It felt like I was opening a window and seeing a view that I had never come across, a break in the cycle.

"Tell us about it," Kivo said.

When I saw my friends walk in through the front door, I didn't really know what they thought they would see. I didn't know if they were expecting to be blown away, because neither of them had really seen the extent of my drawings besides a couple doodles. Maybe they were expecting something a little weird, something straight out of the diary of an emotional boy with a big imagination. One thing I knew for sure though was that they were expecting to see themselves in it.

On the other side of the patio and away from the field of flowers, was a beach under the same pastel sunset. The water was a murky blue by the shore before it transitioned to a clear blue as it neared the horizon. There were wooden fishing boats under tall palm trees, and broken bottles by the sharp rocks on the sand. In the middle of the water was a boat, big and grey with lots of windows and a single light on the very front. I painted the light cutting through the sky, bright and white.

On the beach, were the backs of six people; one girl and five boys, from their short limbs and bright outfits, it was easy enough to make out that they were six young children hold-ing hands in a line as they stared out at the water. I wanted them to pay attention to it and I wanted them to understand why it was important for me to paint them like this. I needed to see if they all felt the same way looking at this, the same kind of emotional tie that I had to it.

"Our clothes," Cassie said first. I had never seen her so speech-less. Her fingers were gently scratching on her other arm and I knew that she was doing it to distract herself from saying or doing anything.

The clothes that I painted on the kids were their favor-ite clothes from when we were younger, the same ones we would wear multiple times a week even though it was stained from rough sword battles between ten-year-olds in the playground. We had never been to that beach when we were little. We never had a spot that we really called our own. The streets of that town were our hideouts. Every grocery store, every restaurant, every ice cream truck—we found magic in everything that was simple and small. The world was so exciting that we didn't have the need to find an escape from it.

"We probably became friends dressed exactly like this," Mitchell said with a grin. He was wearing a red t-shirt with a bright yellow Superman logo on it. He would bring it wherever he went, changing into it whenever they stepped foot onto the playground because he was convinced that it gave him extra strength.

Gryme would always wear a plain black tank top, Kivo with his snapback and a light blue polo shirt and Mo with a white graphic t-shirt that had Scrabble letters printed all over it. Back when Cassie was a kid, she would wear actual dresses. Her favorite one was a light purple sundress with white flowers on it.

We always found it funny that we all wore our favorite outfits to my eleventh birthday party. I had pulled the photo up on my phone to paint the exact details.

"The kids we were back then, we were always on our own little 'escape' beach. You helped me look at everything the way I looked at that ferry in the water. Everything was a possibility. Everything was a new door to be opened."

I remembered that conversation I had with Cassie on the beach, when she asked me what was making me change my opinions about the life I had so much. I finally understood how I had closed myself off from seeing the best in things and I had placed a blindfold around my own eyes because I was scared that the bigger picture wouldn't be as great and exciting as I thought it would be.

"I want us to always remember what it felt like to be those kids. I want us to always feel like we're on that beach, finding something new and making it our own," I paused, wide-eyed as they slowly approached me and wrapped me into a tight group hug. Mo was squeezing the small of my back pretty tightly, and Gryme's face was tucked a little uncomfortably by the side of my neck. Cassie was pushing her way through to wrap her arm around my waist, and Kivo pushed back harder to squeeze his small frame past Gryme. Mitchell just stretched his arms over everyone, not even trying to attempt moving anywhere into this little circle.

It was messy and hilarious. It was child-like but it was the sort of meaningful that a child wouldn't be able to appreciate just yet. It was everything that I loved about this friendship.

"We're always going to be right there with you, Jesse boy," Gryme said.

We spent the next hour talking about the painting of the field of flowers, and I spent some time explaining the situation at home with my mother and how it's really been since Dawson left. I told them about my conversation with Dawson and how I felt that things may start to be different now. I was doing everything I could to let them in as much as they could, to take off that blindfold and find people standing right next to me when I had thought that I had to sort my head out alone the whole time.

I looked over at the mural, pinching myself just to make sure that I wasn't dreaming.

* * *

I had stopped keeping track of time for so long that I didn't know what it would feel like to hope for something not to end.

The whole time I was at the inn, I had never thought of the idea that I would have to eventually leave it and head back home. I was the first one to wake up. The sky wasn't fully bright yet, and the birds were still warming up for their morning songs. I turned from my side and onto my back, my head perched on a pillow that was too soft to be considered hard but too hard to be considered a good one for my neck.

There was something about the thought of leaving that made me feel uneasy, a mix between having butterflies in my stomach and just wanting to outright puke. I couldn't help but take note of the building anxiety in the back of my mind. What if nothing really changed at all once we left? What if it took ages before I could catch myself out of a usual routine again?

I was sleeping right across from the wall that I had painted, but I didn't want to look at it just yet. I kept my eyes fixed on the ceiling. The ceiling fan here didn't make squeaky noises, but it definitely looked much older. There were dust balls hanging off the brown stains on blades that used to be completely white. It moved fast though, and it did a pretty good job at replacing the hot and humid air in the room with the breeze that came through the crack in the window.

I wondered if this was what came after every moment of happiness or content—a sense of longing, a thirst for the next one. For a second, I had the fleeting thought that there was really no point for anyone to enjoy themselves if we were all going to end up sad anyway once we had to say goodbye to something good.

The sun was starting to creep up from behind the trees right in front of the window, strong rays piercing through the glass and spreading across the ceiling and if I squinted my eyes a little I could see colors and thin shapes moving around the sunlight. I had learned in school a couple years back that they were called phosphenes, little sensations that looked like stars or random patterns caused by electric charges produced by the retina in its resting state. I watched them mindlessly drift across the room. Maybe I should be like them, continuously moving on to find the next plain sight that they could make a little more interesting. I smiled at the thought.

I stood up, again creeping my way to the door so I didn't wake anyone. Opening the door, I heard sounds. It was busy downstairs with lots of people crossing the lawn and heading out the gates with their bags. It was the end of the weekend, so I assumed that everyone was getting themselves ready to move on to something else too. The families were getting ready to head back to work and school. The backpackers were getting ready to head home, or head to the next destination on their list of places to travel to. But they all looked so used to it. They didn't look scared.

In the lobby downstairs, I found Dawson sitting on a wooden stool behind the reception desk eating a sandwich. It was probably a sandwich from that morning's new breakfast menu, because it was made with thick artisan bread with a generous serving of meat and cheese wedged between them.

"You look awfully relaxed for a morning with so many guests moving about," I said, crossing my arms on the cool marble of the desk and resting my chin on them. "You're not even wearing your cute little receptionist shirt."

Dawson's eyes widened when he heard my voice, clearly too engrossed in breakfast to notice me walking right up to him. He quickly put the sandwich down and brushed the crumbs off his pale orange tank top. I couldn't help but notice how much younger Dawson looked this morning. He had shaved and his hair was done up, with a child-like innocence surrounding him as he pushed the half-eaten sandwich far behind some piles of log books.

"You paint one wall and you think you're some big shot that can talk about my shirt? No way," Dawson said, coming out from around the desk to give me a sharp jab in the shoulder. "But good morning to you little Jesse, are you all packed up? You don't look awfully relaxed."

"Is it weird that I'm kind of sad," I asked with a sigh, playing with the pens on the desk for guests to fill out paperwork. There were these weird colorful feathers tied onto them with cheap white rubber bands. They did add some personality to the space though, I had to admit.

"Why?"

"These past few days felt so surreal. I was talking about looking at the world like a child again, and finding the magic in everything and all that. But knowing that I'm going back to everything kinda scares me," I lifted my chin up and looked at him, my head still resting on his arms. "I just don't want to let myself and every-one else down. I believe in myself but what if nothing changes?"

"I'm coming back with you guys," Dawson cut me off.

I sprang upright. "You're what?"

"I was thinking about what you told me yesterday, and I asked if I could take some time off to just go home and spend time with you and mom. See the boys again. Think about college maybe, I don't know."

Looking at Dawson in front of me saying this, I was suddenly pulled back to the image of my brother in his school uniform. He looked the same but so different. There was this unexplainable aura around him that made me realize how much he had grown up over the months that he had spent alone. Dawson had long taken off the blind folds that had kept him from seeing the bigger picture.

I couldn't stop myself from rushing forward to give him a tight hug. I did feel embarrassed after realizing that my head still only reached up right below his shoulder.

Dawson laughed and let out a soft "wow" under his breath, slowly wrapping his arms around me and giving it a brief but tight squeeze. It hurt a little, honestly.

"I think I've never thought about the idea of going back because I didn't want to think about the next step, to be reminded about what it felt like to be uncertain about myself," Dawson paused, placing his arms on my shoulder and pushing me a few steps back. "But you reminded me that finding me didn't have to mean losing everyone else. You've grown up a lot, Jesse. I know more than anyone that you're going to be just fine."

** * *

"Let's load the car up!" Gryme called out. Dawson and I were going to be riding with him in his car.

Everyone was out on the lawn, all our bags piled up into a small heap on the grass. It was a little after noon, and the sun was a piercing kind of hot. There were patches of sweat staining the back of all their clothes.

I was about to pick my bags up but two pairs of arms grabbed onto my shoulder and pulled me back a few steps.

"Excuse me?" I said in a daze, regaining my balance only to notice that I was huddled up with my head against Kivo and Mo. "What are you guys doing?"

"We want to know what's going on with Mitchell and Cassie and we're going to ask them right now," Mo said in a harsh whisper. Kivo nodded his head enthusiastically in response.

"I really don't think we should," I said carefully, a little unsure if that was what I wanted but completely sure that it was what Mitchell and Cassie would want. Kivo and Mo had their faces scrunched up into something that I assumed was a pout. I realized that the two of them probably had to deal with Mitchell and Cassie a whole lot more while I was distancing myself from everyone. My own face scrunched up realizing how much I had missed out.

"I can literally hear you guys," Cassie said. The three of us turned around, eyes wide and mouth clamped shut. "We'll talk about it some other time, how about that?" Cassie said with a small smile, motioning for us to get out of our little huddle.

"Look at your face! You're so...soft," Kivo said with a gasp, clutching his hand to his heart. I grabbed him before Cassie could launch forward with a pinch to his stomach. I agreed with Kivo though, Cassie did have a softer expression on her face. It was strange thinking about her and Mitchell hanging out on their own without telling anybody, but I knew Cassie enough to know that she would never risk their friendship if she wasn't comfortable with the idea of it transitioning into something more.

I looked over at Mitchell who was directing everyone to get their bags and stack them up in his trunk so that there would still be enough space for him to fit bags of fruit that he had to buy for his parents on their way home. There were roadside fruit stalls lined up under the trees past the next highway run by local family-run orchards. Mitchell's parents were strongly against the fruits sold at supermarkets. Mitchell was a commanding presence to be around and a big family guy. I found it funny that I had only noticed at this moment just how much of Cassie's type Mitchell actually was.

I flinched a little seeing how Mitchell stopped talking for a second just to glance over at Cassie as she walked past him. It was definitely a lot to take in. Behind him, Mo and Kivo let out little groans under their breath too. "So weird," they whispered in unison.

"Wanna get something to eat before we drop everyone home?" Mitchell asked, swinging his backpack over his shoulder.

"How about that restaurant we all used to go to, the one at that street corner by the playground you guys always chill at," Dawson said.

It was the one that I never went back to after Dawson left. The one where we would watch soccer games until Dawson's friends came and we would all head outside so that the older boys could light their cigarettes up.

"Sure thing, boss," Gryme said, holding his hand up into a salute. Dawson gave Gryme a firm nudge and rolled his eyes.

We were soon done loading all their bags into the car. Kivo had just left with the rest of them in his minivan.

As Gryme pulled out of the driveway, I gazed out at the inn looking at the green lawn, the old brown walls and the black and gold letters. I plugged my earphones in, much to Gryme's dismay at the fact that he was going to have to stay relatively silent for most of the trip. I looked at the car's side mirror, catching my reflection again. I gave myself a small smile, a proud one.

It felt good to recognize myself again.

ACKNOWLEDGMENTS

———

Nothing about writing this book would have been possible without the people around me. There would have been nothing to inspire me. There would have been nothing to make me believe that I could do this. This wasn't a biography, but it was an ode to emotions that were extremely personal and important to me. I want to thank everyone mentioned below for helping me believe that I matter.

To my family, I do everything I do for you. I love you all so much! Thank you for sharing the news of this book with everyone you know, thank you for always checking up on me constantly and thank you for loving me unconditionally.

To my friends (Shout out to Empat), thank you for being a huge inspiration behind the main themes of this book. We've created the most amazing stories and memories together. Thank you for making my youth feel like a movie. I can't wait to watch us grow up and reach out dreams.

My life in San Jose is something I never thought I would have. I would have no way of doing my best out here without the love and support of everyone I spend my days with here. Thank you, Sam, for being my rock through the years and all the years to come - I don't know what I'd do without you. Thank you, Kevin, for making me the happiest I could possibly be.

Thank you to everyone at New Degree Press for being such wonderful mentors throughout this entire process. Everybody that I've worked has inspired me in ways that I can't even describe. You guys are amazing.

And last but not least, thank you to everyone who purchased this book. I want to personally mention everyone else that pre-ordered. I can't thank you all enough.

Jovan Oh	Murali Subramaniam
Ian Chew	Dizeri Mokhtar
The Norris Family	Vivienne Tan
Charanjit Singh	Sheila K

Joel Fluette

Mary Frances

Joey Wong

Kylar Oh

Khadijah Amir

Rachael Wong

Julia Ruggiero

Mike Corpos

Louis Lin

Hannah Amores

Binh Do

Miguel Lopez

Imran Idzqandar

Stanley He

Darlene Tran

Hugo Vera

Anthony Pun

Anthony Ng

Huy Banh

Alysha Ravendran

Ben Stein

CJ Cadiz

Liz Garcia

Hanalyn Menor

Jennifer Wadsworth

Marci Suela

Quoran Houston

Derick Galdamez

Melisa Yuriar

Jackie Contretas

Huan Xun Chan

Garsin Yu

Vivian Pang

Gabriel Mungaray

Luke Johnson

Mike Lin

Tracy Gunapalan

Katheryna Khong

Ryan Teo

Eugene Parra

Steven Nam

Dominoe Ibarra

Bryan Wong

Su Yee Aw

Min You Cheah

Elizabeth Sambath

Vanessa Wong